中国预约定价安排年度报告
China Advance Pricing Arrangement Annual Report

(2020)

中华人民共和国国家税务总局 编

State Taxation Administration People's Republic of China

卷首寄语

　　艰难方显勇毅，磨砺始得玉成。2020年，面对肆虐全球的新冠肺炎疫情和逆势而动的单边主义浪潮，中国"十三五"规划圆满收官，全面建成小康社会取得伟大历史性成就，决战脱贫攻坚取得决定性胜利。站在历史交汇点，国家税务总局坚决贯彻党中央、国务院决策部署，积极拓展国际税收合作，持续深化税收征管体制改革，以昂扬的姿态迎接中国共产党建党一百周年。

　　这一年，受疫情影响，国际商贸往来按下了"暂停键"，经济发展挂上了"倒车挡"，部分国家却滥用泛政治化的"防火墙"，跨境纳税人在单边主义和疫情的夹缝中举步维艰，对税收确定性的期盼与日俱增。值此困局，国家税务总局积极构建合作共赢的国际税收体系，加强新时代国际税收工作。**推进"一带一路"税收征管合作有力度**。举办"同心抗疫，共克时艰"主题线上会议，围绕抗疫情促发展开展广泛交流研讨；组织"一带一路"税收征管合作机制信息化线上高级别会议，达

Preface

Only in hard times can courage and perseverance be manifested and only after polishing can a piece of jade be finer. 2020 was not an easy year for the mankind as almost the whole world, amidst rising unilateralism, was besieged by the Covid-19 pandemic. Even confronted with the unprecedented challenges, China was able to deliver on the 13th Five-Year Plan, marking a historic milestone in the journey of building a moderately prosperous society in all respects and achieving a decisive success in eradicating extreme poverty. Standing at the historic crossroads, the State Taxation Administration (STA), under the guidance of the Central Committee of the Communist Party of China (CPC), has been actively engaged in the international taxation cooperation, while continuing on the deepening of the structural reform on tax collection and administration, in order to prepare for the celebration of the centenary of the founding of the CPC in 2021.

This year, cross-border business and trades had to be suspended and the world economy was dealt with a blow by the COVID-19 outbreak. But there were still a few countries that liked to politicize everything, trying to put the breaks on globalization. The outbreak of the pandemic and the resurgence of unilateralism has made the need for cross-border tax certainty even more urgent for the taxpayers. Rising to the occasion, the STA had made it one of its priorities to building an international tax system that facilitated cooperation and delivered mutually beneficial outcomes.

The STA has deepened the "Belt and Road Initiative" (BRI) cooperation on tax collection and administration. In June, the online conference, "Responding to Covid-19: BRITACOM[1] Perspective", was successfully held, and the participants discussed and exchanged opinions about combating the virus and pushing forward with the development of BRITCOM. At the end of this year, another high-level video conference was organized under the theme of "New Challenges, New Opportunities, New Future—Development Planning of Tax

---

[1] Belt and Road Initiative Tax Administration Cooperation Mechanism.

成15项重要成果；创刊《"一带一路"税收（英文）》杂志，推动税收治理迈上新台阶。**参与国际税收规则调整变革有深度。**参加应对数字经济税收挑战多边共识方案谈判，增强中国在国际税收规则制定中的话语权；译介OECD部分最新指引，并就有关协定执行和非居民业务热点问题进行解答，密切跟进规则变化。**优化税收营商环境服务对外开放有温度。**开展线上相互协商28次，为纳税人消除国际重复征税20亿元；发布（更新）国别（地区）投资指南104份，助力企业了解投资目的地税收政策；落实境外投资者以分配利润直接投资暂不征收预提所得税政策，递延纳税合计106亿元。

作为改善税收营商环境、助力国际税收合作的重要举措之一，中国预约定价安排工作稳步推进，为疫情下的跨境投资提供了更多的税收确定性，更加有效地避免和消除了重复征税，也成为国际税收合作的重要窗口。本书介绍了中国预约定价安排最新税收政策、执行程序及工作开展情况，并对相关统计数据进行了梳理、分析。希望对跨境纳税人了解中国税收环境有所裨益，对社会各界认识与了解预约定价安排工作有所帮助。

中国国家税务总局副局长

Digitalization", with 15 major outcomes delivered. Also, the first edition of *Belt and Road Initiative Tax* journal was released, adding onto the knowledge sharing initiatives taken on by the BRITACOM.

The STA continued to play a key role in the international rule making process. By actively participating in the multilateral negotiation in addressing the tax challenges arising from the digitalization of the economy, the STA has shown its ability in influencing the international tax rule making. Also, the STA has made itself available to address issues arising from the special circumstances caused by the outbreak of the pandemic that are related to treaty implementation and non-resident taxation, while closely following the changes and revisions that have been made to the international standards.

The STA was dedicated to improving the tax environment for businesses as part of China's opening-up policy. The STA had conducted 28 virtual bilateral consultations to eliminate more than 2 billion double taxation for taxpayers. 104 Country (Region) Taxation Guidelines for Cross-Border Investment were released or updated to help taxpayers better understand taxation policies of the investment destinations. Apart from that, the policy that provided for temporary exemption on withholding tax for foreign investors that directly invested the distributed profits in the businesses was consistently implemented, saving 10.6 billion for taxpayers in the form of deferred taxes.

As one of the measures taken by the STA to improve the business environment and boost international taxation cooperation, China's APA program, which was put in place to prevent double taxation and support cross-border investments and trades, has been running on a steady pace. This report continues to offer information on relevant tax policies, implementation procedures and development of China's APA program. Statistics on the program is also provided for analytical purposes. The STA expects the report to help cross-border taxpayers as well as the general public better understand China's taxation environment and APA program.

WANG Daoshu
The Deputy Commissioner
State Taxation Administration

目 录

说明 ··· 2

一、预约定价安排概况 ·· 6
    （一）概念 ·· 6
    （二）分类 ·· 6
    （三）优势 ·· 6

二、预约定价安排立法与实践发展 ···································· 10
    （一）发展历程 ··· 10
    （二）现行法规依据（截至2021年8月）··························· 14

三、预约定价安排操作规范 ··· 16
    （一）申请资格 ··· 16
    （二）操作流程 ··· 16
        1. 预备会谈 ·· 20
        2. 谈签意向 ·· 22
        3. 分析评估 ·· 24
        4. 正式申请 ·· 26
        5. 协商签署 ·· 28
        6. 监控执行 ·· 30

Contents

Notes ... 3

I Introduction to China's APA Program ... 7

    1. Definition ... 7

    2. Categorization ... 7

    3. Advantages ... 7

II Legislation and Practice Development of China's APA ... 11

    1. History ... 11

    2. Existing Legal and Regulatory Basis (by August 2021) ... 15

III APA Procedures ... 17

    1. Prerequisites to an APA Application ... 17

    2. APA Process and Implementation ... 17

        A. Pre-filing Meeting ... 21

        B. Letter of Intent ... 23

        C. Analysis and Evaluation ... 25

        D. Formal Application ... 27

        E. Negotiation and Signing ... 29

        F. Implementation and Monitoring ... 31

目 录

　　（三）追溯调整 …………………………………………………………… 32
　　（四）续签 ………………………………………………………………… 34
　　（五）暂停或终止 ………………………………………………………… 34
　　（六）涉及多个税务机关的情况 ………………………………………… 36

四、单边预约定价安排简易程序操作规范 ……………………………………… 38
　　（一）申请及适用年度 …………………………………………………… 38
　　　　1. 申请资格 …………………………………………………………… 38
　　　　2. 适用年度 …………………………………………………………… 38
　　（二）操作流程 …………………………………………………………… 38
　　　　1. 申请评估 …………………………………………………………… 40
　　　　2. 协商签署 …………………………………………………………… 42
　　　　3. 监控执行 …………………………………………………………… 44
　　（三）其他事项 …………………………………………………………… 44

五、预约定价安排中纳税人权利保障 …………………………………………… 46
　　（一）纳税人信息保密 …………………………………………………… 46
　　（二）纳税人缔约自由 …………………………………………………… 46

六、预约定价安排统计数据 ……………………………………………………… 48
　　（一）预约定价安排年度分布 …………………………………………… 48
　　（二）预约定价安排谈签阶段分布 ……………………………………… 52
　　（三）预约定价安排交易类型分布 ……………………………………… 52
　　（四）双边预约定价安排区域分布 ……………………………………… 54
　　（五）预约定价安排完成时间 …………………………………………… 56
　　（六）预约定价安排使用的转让定价方法 ……………………………… 58
　　（七）预约定价安排涉及的行业 ………………………………………… 62

七、预约定价安排申请联系人信息 ……………………………………………… 64

3. Rollback ··· 33

　　　4. Renewal ··· 35

　　　5. Termination or Cancellation ··· 35

　　　6. Particular Situations Referred to Multiple Tax Authorities ··················· 37

IV The Simplified Procedure for UAPA ·· **39**

　　　1. Prerequisites and Tax Years to be Covered by UAPA Simplified Procedure ············ 39

　　　　　(1) Prerequisites ·· 39

　　　　　(2) Tax Years to be Covered by UAPA Simplified Procedure ············ 39

　　　2. The Process of UAPA Simplified Procedure ·· 39

　　　　　A. Application and Evaluation ··· 41

　　　　　B. Negotiation and Signing ··· 43

　　　　　C. Implementation and Monitoring ·· 45

　　　3. Other Issues ··· 45

V Protection of Taxpayers' Rights ··· **47**

　　　1. Confidentiality of Taxpayers' Information ··· 47

　　　2. Taxpayers' Freedom of Contract ·· 47

VI APA Statistics ·· **49**

　　　1. APAs Signed by Year ·· 49

　　　2. APAs by Phase ·· 53

　　　3. APAs by Transaction Type ··· 53

　　　4. Bilateral APAs by Region ··· 55

　　　5. APAs by Time Taken ·· 57

　　　6. APAs by Transfer Pricing Method ··· 59

　　　7. Industries Covered by Signed APAs ·· 63

VII STA Contacts (by Province) for APA Requests ··· **65**

目 录

附录：预约定价安排表证单书 ……………………………………… 70
    1. 预约定价安排预备会谈申请书 …………………………………… 70
    2. 预约定价安排谈签意向书 ………………………………………… 72
    3. 预约定价安排正式申请书 ………………………………………… 74
    4. 单边预约定价安排 ………………………………………………… 76
    5. 预约定价安排补（退）税款通知书 ……………………………… 82
    6. 预约定价安排续签申请书 ………………………………………… 84
    7. 启动特别纳税调整相互协商程序申请表 ………………………… 86
    8. 单边预约定价安排简易程序申请书 ……………………………… 90

Appendices: Forms and Schedules of the APA Program **71**

    1. APA Pre-filing Meeting Application Letter 71

    2. APA Letter of Intent 73

    3. APA Formal Application Letter 75

    4. Advance Pricing Arrangement (Unilateral) (Text for Reference) 77

    5. Notice on APA Tax Payable (Refundable) 83

    6. APA Renewal Application 85

    7. Application to Initiate Transfer Pricing Mutual Agreement Procedures 87

    8. Application Letter for the Simplified Procedure for UAPA 91

说 明

本报告是中华人民共和国国家税务总局第十二次发布的预约定价安排年度报告，旨在介绍中国预约定价安排最新制度、程序、数据及实施情况，为有意与中国税务机关达成预约定价安排的企业提供指导，也为其他国家和地区[①]税务主管当局及社会各界了解中国预约定价安排工作提供参考。本报告不具有法律效力，不应作为企业及中国税务机关谈签预约定价安排的依据。

本报告统计数据涵盖的时间范围为2005年1月1日至2020年12月31日。

截至2020年12月31日，中国税务机关已累计签署116例单边预约定价安排和90例双边预约定价安排。

2020年签署15例单边预约定价安排和14例双边预约定价安排。在签署的双边预约定价安排中，与亚洲国家（地区）签署9例，与北美洲国家签署2例，与欧洲国家签署2例，与大洋洲国家签署1例。制造业的预约定价安排仍是主体，凸显了税收服务实体经济的作用。

---

① 本报告提及的国家和地区是指拥有独立税收管辖权的国家和地区。

Notes

This is the 12nd APA annual report released by the State Taxation Administration (STA) to describe the latest mechanisms, procedures, and implementation of the APA program in China. This report is intended to provide guidance to enterprises interested in entering into APAs with the Chinese tax authority, and to serve as a reference for competent authorities of other countries (regions) and the general public to better understand China's APA program. It does not have legal validity, and therefore should not be regarded as a legal basis for enterprises or the Chinese tax authority to negotiate or conclude an APA.

This report contains data pertaining to period between January 1, 2005 and December 31, 2020.

By December 31, 2020, the cumulative total of APAs signed is 206, 116 unilateral and 90 bilateral.

In 2020, a total of 15 unilateral APAs and 14 bilateral APAs were signed. Of the 14 bilateral APAs, 9 were signed with Asian countries (regions), 2 were signed with North American countries, 2 were signed with European countries and the remaining 1 was signed with an Oceanian country. Most of the APAs signed in 2020 still involve manufacturing industry, which demonstrates the role of taxation on serving the real economy.

作为税基侵蚀和利润转移（BEPS）成果落实项目，《特别纳税调查调整及相互协商程序管理办法》（国家税务总局公告2017年第6号发布，以下简称6号公告）和《关于预约定价安排管理有关事项的公告》（国家税务总局公告2016年第64号，以下简称64号公告）共同为预约定价安排事项提供了法律依据和过程指导。2021年，为进一步优化营商环境，提升单边预约定价安排谈签效率，国家税务总局颁布了《关于单边预约定价安排适用简易程序有关事项的公告》（国家税务总局公告2021年第24号，以下简称24号公告）。为了给纳税人提供及时、有效的指导，以便其了解最新的预约定价安排制度和程序，本报告将24号公告内容收录。

为落实BEPS第5项行动计划最低标准的要求，2016年4月1日以后签署的单边预约定价安排被纳入强制自发情报交换框架。

随着BEPS行动计划的推进和各国税务机关对反避税管理的加强，预计未来预约定价安排申请也将逐步增加。税务机关将继续严把申请关，在决定是否优先受理企业申请时主要考虑以下因素：① 企业提交申请的时间顺序。② 所提交申请的质量，例如，材料是否齐备，是否提供足够资料清晰证明整个价值链或供应链的交易情况，预约定价安排拟采用的定价原则和计算方法是否合理等。对于不符合要求的申请，要求企业进行补充完善。③ 案件是否具有行业和区域等方面的特殊性。④ 对于双边预约定价安排申请，还需考虑案件所涉对方国家（地区）的谈签意愿及其对案件的重视程度。在上述四个因素中，最需要强调的是企业提交申请的质量。如果所提交的申请有创新方法，有高质量的关于无形资产、成本节约或市场溢价的量化分析，则会得到优先处理。其他考虑因素在64号公告和下文中均有具体说明。

As the implementation programme of BEPS action plans, the *Public Notice of the State Taxation Administration on Issuing the Administrative Measures for Special Tax Adjustment and Investigation and Mutual Agreement Procedures* (Public Notice of the State Taxation Administration〔2017〕No. 6, hereinafter referred to as Public Notice No. 6) and *Public Notice on Matters Regarding Enhancing the Administration of Advance Pricing Arrangements* (Public Notice of the State Taxation Administration〔2016〕No. 64, hereinafter referred to as the Public Notice No. 64) jointly provide regulatory basis and process guidance for APA matters. In order to optimize business environment and make the process of unilateral APA more efficiently, the STA releases *Public Notice of the State Taxation Administration on Matters Regarding the Application of the Simplified Procedure for Unilateral Advance Pricing Arrangements* (Public Notice of the State Taxation Administration〔2021〕No. 24, hereinafter referred to as Public Notice No. 24). The Public Notice No. 24 is included in this report to provide timely and effective guidance for taxpayers so as to help them understand the lastest system and procedure of APA.

Required by the BEPS Action 5 minimum standard, the unilateral APAs signed after April 1, 2016 are subject to the compulsory spontaneous exchange framework.

It is expected that the APA request will arise against the backdrop of concern about uncertainty drawn out by the universal implementation of BEPS projects and the increased transfer pricing scrutiny by tax administrations. The STA has therefore determined to prioritize certain APA requests, taking into account the following factors:

a) Overall principle: first come, first served. b) The quality of the request submission, e.g. whether all required documents have been submitted, whether sufficient documentation clearly evidencing the transactions throughout the entire value chain or supply chain has been provided, whether the applied transfer pricing method is appropriate, and whether the calculation is correct. Applicant will be required to make additions or revisions to the submission when necessary. c) Whether the applicant is in a specific industry or located in a specific region that merits prioritized attention. d) For a BAPA request, whether the BAPA partner country (region) has the intention to accept the case and pursue the BAPA will also be an important factor for consideration. Among the four factors, the one the STA values most is the quality of the submission. A submission that presents innovative application of transfer pricing methods or high quality quantitative analysis for intangibles, cost savings or market premiums will merit the STA's prioritized attention.

一、预约定价安排概况

（一）概　念

预约定价安排，是指企业就其未来年度关联交易的定价原则和计算方法，向税务机关提出申请，与税务机关按照独立交易原则协商、确认后达成的协议。预约定价安排适用于主管税务机关向企业送达接收其谈签意向的《税务事项通知书》之日所属纳税年度起3至5个年度的关联交易。

（二）分　类

预约定价安排按照参与的国家（地区）税务主管当局的数量，可以分为单边、双边和多边三种类型。

企业与一国税务机关签署的预约定价安排为单边预约定价安排。单边预约定价安排只能为企业提供一国内关联交易定价原则和计算方法的确定性，而不能有效规避企业境外关联方被其所在国家（地区）的税务机关进行转让定价调查调整的风险。因此，单边预约定价安排无法避免或消除国际重复征税。

企业与两个或两个以上国家（地区）税务主管当局签署的预约定价安排为双边或多边预约定价安排，需要税务主管当局之间就企业跨境关联交易的定价原则和计算方法达成一致，可以有效避免或消除国际重复征税，为企业转让定价问题提供确定性。

（三）优　势

预约定价安排是税务机关和企业通过合作的方式处理企业转让定价问题以及潜在转让定

I Introduction to China's APA Program

1. Definition

An APA refers to an arrangement whereby an enterprise applies in advance to negotiate and reach agreement with the tax authorities in respect of the transfer pricing methods and corresponding calculation methods to be applied to its related party transactions for future years in accordance with the arm's length principle. An APA applies to related party transactions over a period of 3 to 5 consecutive years starting from the year during which *Notice on Tax Matters* is issued by the in-charge tax administration(s) notifying the acceptance of enterprise's intent for the APA.

2. Categorization

An APA may be categorized as unilateral, bilateral or multilateral based on the number of competent authorities involved in the APA.

In a unilateral APA, the enterprise enters into the APA with one country's tax authority. A unilateral APA can only provide certainty to the enterprise's pricing methodologies and calculation process with respect to its related party transactions within one country (region), but cannot ensure the effective avoidance of transfer pricing audits or adjustments from the tax authority of the overseas related party(ies) it transact with. Thus, a unilateral APA cannot prevent international double taxation.

In a bilateral or multilateral APA, the enterprise negotiates and enters into the APA with two or more countries' competent authorities. These authorities will need to reach an agreement with regard to the pricing methodologies and calculation process used in the cross-border related party transactions of the enterprise in question. Bilateral and multilateral APAs can be used to effectively avoid international double taxation and provide certainty regarding the transfer pricing policies of the enterprise.

3. Advantages

An APA is an effective approach to deal with transfer pricing issues and potential transfer pricing disputes through the collaboration between tax authorities and an enterprise. An APA between the tax authority (ies) and the enterprise(s) is binding on all parties. The enterprise shall proactively conform to all the provisions

价争议的有效手段。税务机关与企业达成的预约定价安排，对双方均具有约束力。企业应主动遵守安排的全部条款及要求；税务机关应依照安排，做好监控执行工作。

预约定价安排是在税企双方自愿、平等、互信的基础上达成的协议，是税务机关为企业提供的服务，为税企双方增进理解、加强合作、减少对抗提供了有效途径。预约定价安排具有如下优势：

1. 为企业未来年度的转让定价问题提供确定性，从而带来企业经营及税收的确定性，也为税务机关带来稳定的收入预期；

2. 降低税务机关转让定价管理及调查的成本，有效避免企业被税务机关转让定价调查的风险，降低企业的税收遵从成本；

3. 有助于提高税务机关的纳税服务水平，促进税收管理与服务的均衡发展，保障纳税人相关权益的实现。

此外，双边或者多边预约定价安排还特别具备以下优势：

1. 促进各国税务主管当局之间的交流与合作；

2. 使企业可以在两个或两个以上国家（地区）避免被转让定价调整的风险，并有效避免或消除国际重复征税。

and requirements of the arrangement, while tax authority(ies) shall monitor the implementation of the agreement.

An APA is a voluntary agreement conducted on the basis of equality and mutual trust. It serves as an effective mechanism to enhance understanding, strengthen collaboration, and mitigate disputes between enterprises and tax authorities. APAs have the following benefits:

(1) Provide certainty for tax authorities and enterprises in regards to transfer pricing issues for future years, and hence will offer certainty with regard to taxpayers' operations and relevant tax obligations and provide tax authorities with an expectation of steady tax revenue inflows;

(2) Reduce tax authorities' costs related to transfer pricing administration and audit as well as enterprises'tax compliance costs by mitigating the risk of a transfer pricing audit;

(3) Improve the quality of tax compliance services provided by the tax authorities, facilitate the balanced development of administration and service, and assure taxpayers of the relevant rights and benefits.

Bilateral and multilateral APAs can also provide the following advantages:

(1) Facilitate communication and collaboration among the competent tax authorities of different jurisdictions;

(2) Help enterprises avoid transfer pricing adjustments as well as double taxation risks in two (for bilateral APA) or more (for multilateral APA) tax jurisdictions.

二、预约定价安排立法与实践发展

（一）发展历程

中国自20世纪90年代末开始预约定价安排的实践。1998年，预约定价安排作为"转让定价调整方法中的其他合理方法"写入《关联企业间业务往来税务管理规程（试行）》（国税发〔1998〕59号印发）第二十八条[①]。1998年税务机关与企业签署首例单边预约定价安排。

2002年，《中华人民共和国税收征收管理法实施细则》（国务院令第362号公布）第五十三条[②]正式列入预约定价制度，预约定价由转让定价的调整方法上升为一种制度。

2004年，国家税务总局颁布了《关联企业间业务往来预约定价实施规则（试行）》（国税发〔2004〕118号印发），对预约定价安排谈签步骤、要求及后续监控执行等具体操作程序做出详细规定，从而规范了中国的预约定价安排管理。1998—2004年，中国一些地方税务机关尝试与企业达成一些单边预约定价安排。在这一阶段，由于缺乏全国统一的具体操作规范，各地达成的预约定价安排普遍存在条款过于简化、功能风险分析和可比性分析不足等问题，为此，本报告的统计数据并没有包括这一阶段签署的预约定价安排。

2005年，为促进全国预约定价管理工作的规范统一，国家税务总局实施了预约定价监控管理制度，即各地税务机关在签署单边预约定价安排前必须逐级层报税务总局审核，同时要求各地税务机关要稳步推进预约定价工作，严格依据有关规定，提高预约定价安排的规范程度。中国的预约定价管理从此步入了规范发展的新阶段。2005年4月19日，中国与日本签署了我国历史上第一例双边预约定价安排。随后，中国分别于2007年4月20日和11月17日与美国、韩国相继达成了双方历史上的首例双边预约定价安排。2005—2008年4年间，税务机关

[①] "**第二十八条** 有形财产购销业务转让定价的调整方法。

"……

"（四）其他合理的方法。在上述三种调整方法均不能适用时，可采用其他合理的替代方法进行调整，如可比利润法、利润分割法、净利润法等。经企业申请，主管税务机关批准，也可采用预约定价方法。"

[②] "**第五十三条** 纳税人可以向主管税务机关提出与其关联企业之间业务往来的定价原则和计算方法，主管税务机关审核、批准后，与纳税人预先约定有关定价事项，监督纳税人执行。"

II Legislation and Practice Development of China's APA

1. History

China began using APAs on a trial basis in the late 1990s. In 1998, an APA was included as one of "other reasonable methods of transfer pricing adjustments" in Article 28 of *The Regulation on the Taxation of Transactions between Related Parties (Trial)*[①] (Guo Shui Fa [1998] No. 59). In 1998, the first unilateral APA was reached between the tax authority and an enterprise.

In 2002, the APA program was formally introduced in Article 53 of *Rules for the Implementation of the Law of the People's Republic of China on the Administration of Tax Collection*[②] (Decree No. 362 of the State Council), and APAs were elevated from an adjustment method to a program.

In 2004, the STA promulgated *Implementation Rules on Advance Pricing Arrangements for Transactions between Related Parties (Trial Version)* (Guo Shui Fa [2004] No. 118), which provides details of the APA program and specific procedures such as negotiation and conclusion procedures, requirements, follow-up execution and monitoring, as well as guidance on APA administration in China. Such a step further regulated the administration of China's APA program. From 1998 to 2004, a number of local Chinese tax authorities have attempted to negotiate and conclude several unilateral APAs with taxpayers on a trial basis. However, due to the absence of nationwide standardized and clearly defined implementation guidance, overly-simplified APA articles, insufficient functional and risk analysis and inadequate comparability analysis were found to be prevalent in APAs concluded during the period. For this reason, this report does not contain statistics on APAs concluded during this period.

In order to standardize and ensure consistency of China's APA administration across the country, the STA has implemented rules for APA monitoring and administration since 2005 requiring the local tax authorities to submit the draft unilateral agreement to the STA for review and approval before its conclusion.

---

① Article 28 Transfer Pricing Adjustment Methods for Purchases and Sales of Tangible Assets:
...
(IV) Other appropriate methods: If none of the first three methods are applicable, the tax authorities can choose other reasonable methods, such as "profit-comparison method" "profit-split method" and "net profit method", among others. The enterprise can also adopt an "advance pricing arrangement" after applying for and obtaining approval from the tax bureau in charge...

② Article 53 The taxpayer may propose a pricing principle and calculation method to the in-charge tax authority concerning the transactions between them and associated enterprises. The in-charge tax authority shall examine, verify and decide whether to approve the proposal. If approval is given, an advance agreement shall be reached with the taxpayer concerning pricing related matters and the tax authority shall supervise the implementation.

与企业共签署预约定价安排41例,其中单边预约定价安排36例、双边预约定价安排5例。

2009年,为配合新修订的《中华人民共和国企业所得税法》及其实施条例的实施,国家税务总局颁布实施了《特别纳税调整实施办法(试行)》(国税发〔2009〕2号印发),其中第六章进一步明确了中国预约定价安排制度及操作规范,并首次制定了双边预约定价安排的谈签程序及具体规定。2009年10月26日,中国与丹麦签署第一例双边预约定价安排,开启了我国与欧洲国家反避税双边合作的先河。2009年,双边预约定价安排谈签工作有了较快的发展,全年共签署预约定价安排12例,其中单边预约定价安排5例,双边预约定价安排7例。

2010年,全年共签署预约定价安排8例,其中单边预约定价安排4例,双边预约定价安排4例。

2011年,全年共签署预约定价安排12例,其中单边预约定价安排8例,双边预约定价安排4例。2011年12月29日,我国与新加坡签署两国首例双边预约定价安排。

2012年,全年共签署预约定价安排12例,其中单边预约定价安排3例,双边预约定价安排9例。

2013年,全年共签署预约定价安排19例,其中单边预约定价安排11例,双边预约定价安排8例。

2014年,全年共签署预约定价安排9例,其中单边预约定价安排3例,双边预约定价安排6例。2014年12月5日,我国与瑞士签署两国首例双边预约定价安排。

2015年,全年共签署预约定价安排12例,其中单边预约定价安排6例,双边预约定价安排6例。

2016年,为落实税基侵蚀和利润转移(BEPS)行动计划成果、完善预约定价安排工作流程,国家税务总局颁布实施了《关于完善预约定价安排管理有关事项的公告》(国家税务总局公告2016年第64号)。2016年全年共签署预约定价安排14例,其中单边预约定价安排8例,双边预约定价安排6例。

2017年3月,为践行BEPS第14项行动计划争端解决机制最低标准的相关要求,提高相互协商程序结案效率,积极为纳税人消除国际重复征税,国家税务总局颁布实施了《关于发布〈特别纳税调查调整及相互协商程序管理办法〉的公告》(国家税务总局公告2017年

Meanwhile, local tax authorities are required to steadily promote APA programs and strictly conform to the relevant regulations to improve the administration of the APA program. The program has since entered into a well-regulated time. On April 19, 2005, China and Japan signed China's first bilateral APA. Subsequently, China reached the first bilateral APA with the United States and the Republic of Korea on April 20, 2007 and November 17, 2007 respectively. From 2005 to 2008, the Chinese tax authorities concluded 41 APAs, including 36 unilateral and 5 bilateral APAs.

At the beginning of 2009, *Implementation Measures of Special Tax Adjustments (Trial Version)* (Guo Shui Fa〔2009〕No. 2, hereinafter referred to as the Measures) was promulgated to facilitate the implementation of the *Law of the People's Republic of China on Enterprise Income Tax* and its Implementation Regulations. Chapter Six of the Measures provides more detailed rules and implementation guidance on China's APA program. On October 26, 2009, China signed the first bilateral APA with the Kingdom of Denmark, marking the start of bilateral cooperation between China and European countries in the transfer pricing area. In 2009, China's bilateral APA program began to gain significant momentum with 12 APAs (including 5 unilateral and 7 bilateral) being signed in the year.

In 2010, the Chinese tax authorities signed 8 APAs in total, including 4 unilateral APAs and 4 bilateral APAs.

In 2011, the Chinese tax authorities signed 12 APAs in total, including 8 unilateral APAs and 4 bilateral APAs. On December 29, China signed the first bilateral APA with the Republic of Singapore.

In 2012, the Chinese tax authorities signed 12 APAs in total, including 3 unilateral APAs and 9 bilateral APAs.

In 2013, the Chinese tax authorities signed 19 APAs in total, including 11 unilateral APAs and 8 bilateral APAs.

In 2014, the Chinese tax authorities signed 9 APAs in total, including 3 unilateral APAs and 6 bilateral APAs. On December 5, China signed the first bilateral APA with the Swiss Confederation.

In 2015, the Chinese tax authorities signed 12 APAs in total, including 6 unilateral APAs and 6 bilateral APAs.

In 2016, the Chinese tax authorities signed 14 APAs in total, including 8 unilateral APAs and 6 bilateral APAs. In October, The STA issued the Public Notice No. 64 aiming at implementing the achievements of BEPS project and streamlining the APA workflow.

In 2017, the Chinese tax authorities signed 8 APAs in total, including 3 unilateral APAs and 5 bilateral APAs. In March, in order to incorporate measures recommended by the BEPS Action 14 which requires participating jurisdictions to increase efficiency of resolving MAP cases to eliminate double taxation, the

第6号)。2017年全年共签署预约定价安排8例,其中单边预约定价安排3例,双边预约定价安排5例。

2018年,全年共签署预约定价安排9例,其中单边预约定价安排2例,双边预约定价安排7例。

2019年,全年共签署预约定价安排21例,其中单边预约定价安排12例,双边预约定价安排9例。

2020年,全年共签署预约定价安排29例,其中单边预约定价安排15例,双边预约定价安排14例。

2021年7月,为便利企业获得转让定价税收确定性,助力其在华持续经营,国家税务总局颁布《关于单边预约定价安排适用简易程序有关事项的公告》(国家税务总局公告2021年第24号)。

(二)现行法规依据(截至2021年8月)

中国现行预约定价安排的法律法规及规范性文件主要包括以下内容:

1. 中国政府与其他国家(地区)政府签署的避免双重征税协定、协议或者安排(以下简称税收协定)的相关规定;

2.《中华人民共和国企业所得税法》第四十二条;

3.《中华人民共和国企业所得税法实施条例》第一百一十三条;

4.《中华人民共和国税收征收管理法实施细则》第五十三条;

5.《国家税务总局关于完善预约定价安排管理有关事项的公告》(国家税务总局公告2016年第64号);

6.《国家税务总局关于发布〈特别纳税调查调整及相互协商程序管理办法〉的公告》(国家税务总局公告2017年第6号)。

7.《国家税务总局关于单边预约定价安排适用简易程序有关事项的公告》(国家税务总局公告2021年第24号)。

STA issued the Public Notice No. 6.

In 2018, the Chinese tax authorities signed 9 APAs in total, including 2 unilateral APAs and 7 bilateral APAs.

In 2019, the Chinese tax authorities signed 21 APAs in total, including 12 unilateral APAs and 9 bilateral APAs.

In 2020, the Chinese tax authorities signed 29 APAs in total, including 15 unilateral APAs and 14 bilateral APAs.

In 2021, the *Public Notice of the State Taxation Administration on Matters Regarding Application of the Simplified Procedures for Unilateral Advance Pricing Arrangements* (Public Notice of the State Taxation Administration〔2021〕No. 24) was released to help taxpayers obtain tax certainty.

2. Existing Legal and Regulatory Basis (by August 2021)

The legal basis and relevant laws, regulations and regulatory documents governing APAs primarily include the following:

(1) The relevant clauses in the treaties, agreements or arrangements for the avoidance of double taxation (hereinafter referred to as tax treaty,) between the government of China and the government of the corresponding country (region);

(2) Article 42 of the *Law of the People's Republic of China on Enterprise Income Tax*;

(3) Article 113 of the *Regulations for the Implementation of the Law of the People's Republic of China on Enterprise Income Tax*;

(4) Article 53 of the *Rules for the Implementation of the Law of the People's Republic of China on the Administration of Tax Collection*;

(5) *Public Notice of the State Taxation Administration on Matters Regarding Enhancing the Administration of Advance Pricing Arrangements* (Public Notice of the State Taxation Administration〔2016〕No. 64);

(6) *Public Notice of the State Taxation Administration on Issuing the Administrative Measures for Special Tax Adjustment and Investigation and Mutual Agreement Procedures* (Public Notice of the State Taxation Administration〔2017〕No. 6).

(7) *Public Notice of the State Taxation Administration on Matters Regarding Application of the Simplified Procedures for Unilateral Advance Pricing Arrangements* (Public Notice of the State Taxation Administration〔2021〕No. 24).

三、预约定价安排操作规范[①]

（一）申请资格

预约定价安排一般适用于主管税务机关向企业送达接收其谈签意向的《税务事项通知书》之日所属纳税年度前3个年度每年度发生的关联交易金额4000万元人民币以上的企业。

有下列情形之一的，税务机关可以优先受理企业提交的申请：

1. 企业关联申报和同期资料完备合理，披露充分；
2. 企业纳税信用级别为A级；
3. 税务机关曾经对企业实施特别纳税调查调整，并已经结案；
4. 签署的预约定价安排执行期满，企业申请续签，且预约定价安排所述事实和经营环境没有发生实质性变化；
5. 企业提交的申请材料齐备，对价值链或者供应链的分析完整、清晰，充分考虑成本节约、市场溢价等地域特殊因素，拟采用的定价原则和计算方法合理；
6. 企业积极配合税务机关开展预约定价安排谈签工作；
7. 申请双边或者多边预约定价安排的，所涉及的税收协定缔约对方税务主管当局有较强的谈签意愿，对预约定价安排的重视程度较高；
8. 其他有利于预约定价安排谈签的因素。

（二）操作流程

预约定价安排的谈签和执行经过预备会谈、谈签意向、分析评估、正式申请、协商签署和监控执行6个阶段。预约定价谈签流程见图3-1。

[①] 适用于双边预约定价安排及单边预约定价安排一般程序。

III APA Procedures[1]

1. Prerequisites to an APA Application

Access to APA is available to enterprises with annual related party transaction amount exceeding RMB 40 million for the three years prior to the year in which the *Notice on Tax Matters* is issued by the in-charge tax administration(s) notifying the acceptance of enterprise's intent for the APA.

The tax administration(s) may prioritize APA requests from the enterprise that meets one of the following conditions.

(1) The enterprise's annual reporting forms for related party dealings and contemporaneous transfer pricing documentation are well completed with adequate disclosures.

(2) The enterprise's tax compliance rating is "A".

(3) The enterprise was once under special tax adjustment investigation and the investigation was closed.

(4) The enterprise is applying for a renewal of an existing APA that is about to expire provided that there has been no substantial changes to the facts and operating environment specified in the existing APA.

(5) For the APA request, the enterprise has provided complete and adequate information including but not limited to clear and thorough value chain/supply chain analysis taking into account of location specific advantages such as cost savings and market premium, and appropriate pricing methodologies and calculation process.

(6) The enterprise has been cooperative with the tax administration(s) during the APA process.

(7) For a bilateral/multilateral APA, the competent authority(ies) of the other contracting state(s) of treaty(ies) have displayed strong intention to move forward with the APA negotiation or attached a high importance to the APA.

(8) Any other factors facilitating the APA process is present.

2. APA Process and Implementation

APA process involves the following six stages: pre-filing meeting, letter of intent, analysis and evaluation, formal application, negotiation and signing, and implementation and monitoring (see Chart 3-1).

---

[1] The APA procedure here refers to general procedure excluding the UAPA simplified procedure.

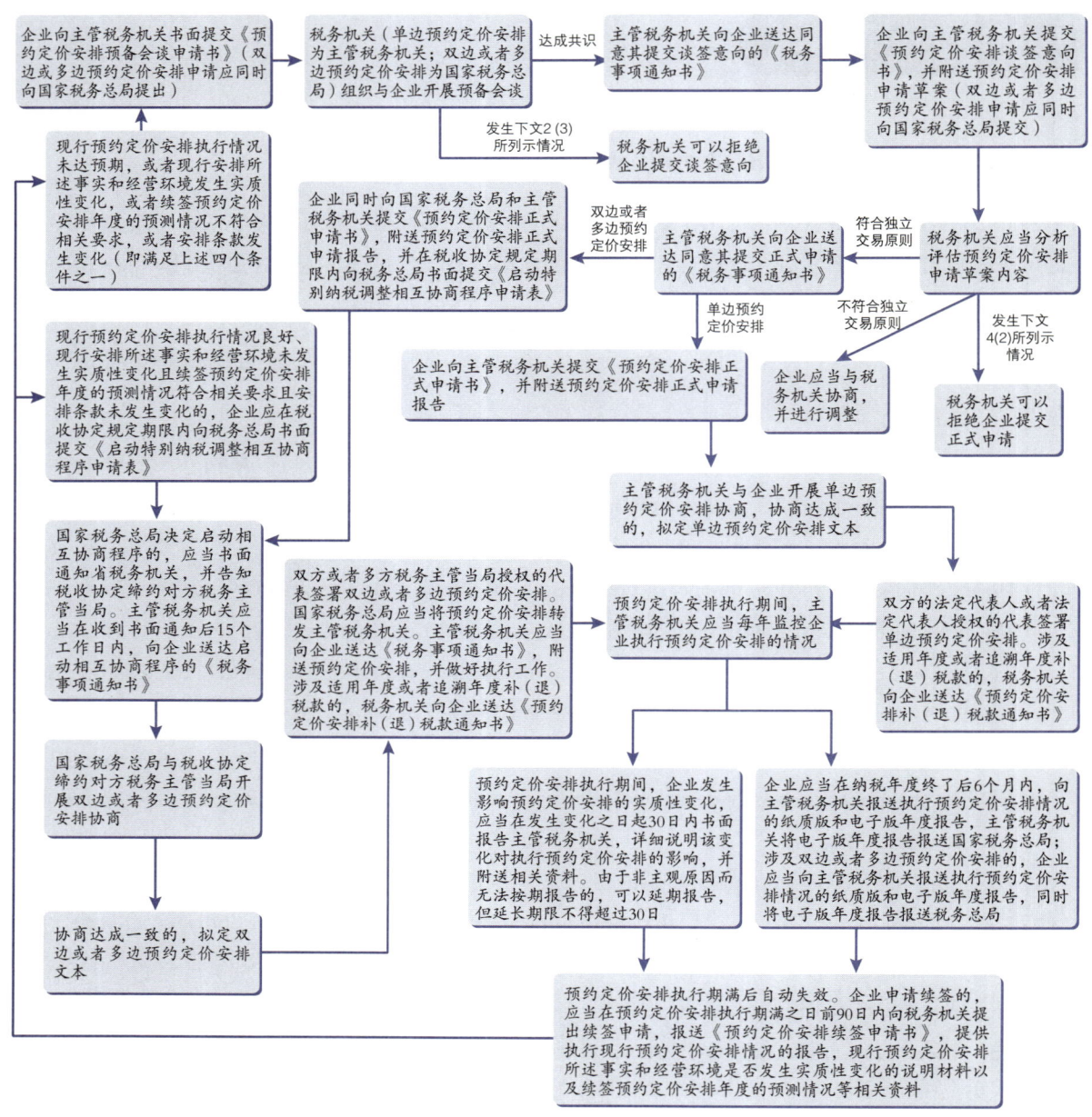

图3-1 预约定价安排谈签流程

China Advance Pricing Arrangement Annual Report (2020)

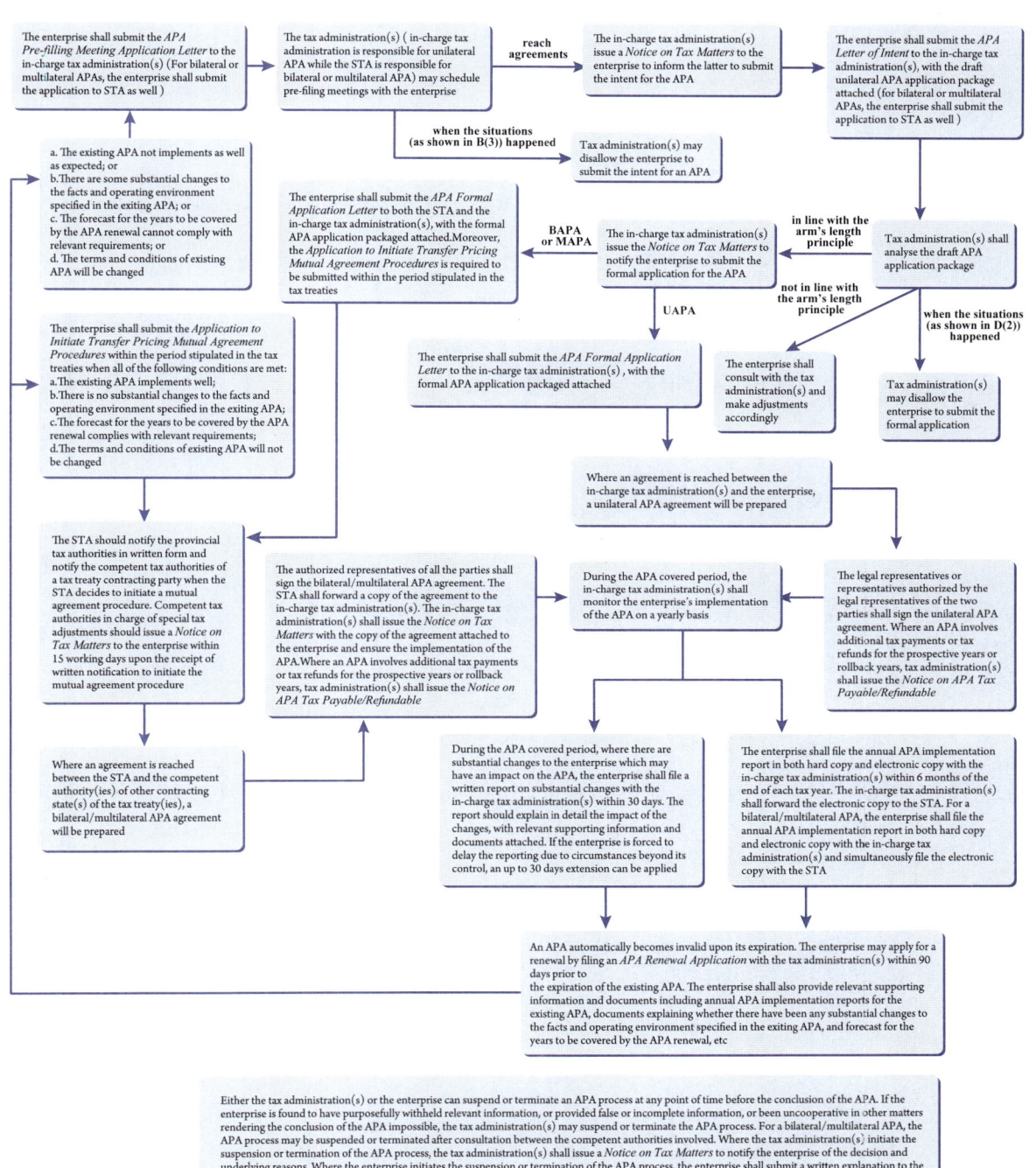

Chart 3-1　The APA Process

1. 预备会谈

企业有谈签预约定价安排意向的，应当向税务机关书面提出预备会谈申请。税务机关可以与企业开展预备会谈。

（1）企业申请单边预约定价安排的，应当向主管税务机关书面提出预备会谈申请，提交《预约定价安排预备会谈申请书》。主管税务机关组织与企业开展预备会谈。

企业申请双边或者多边预约定价安排的，应当同时向国家税务总局和主管税务机关书面提出预备会谈申请，提交《预约定价安排预备会谈申请书》。国家税务总局统一组织与企业开展预备会谈。

（2）预备会谈期间，企业应当就以下内容作出简要说明：

- 预约定价安排的适用年度；
- 预约定价安排涉及的关联方及关联交易；
- 企业及其所属企业集团的组织结构和管理架构；
- 企业最近3至5个年度生产经营情况、同期资料等；
- 预约定价安排涉及各关联方功能和风险的说明，包括功能和风险划分所依据的机构、人员、费用、资产等；
- 市场情况的说明，包括行业发展趋势和竞争环境等；
- 是否存在成本节约、市场溢价等地域特殊优势；
- 预约定价安排是否追溯适用以前年度；
- 其他需要说明的情况。

企业申请双边或者多边预约定价安排的，说明内容还应当包括：

- 向税收协定缔约对方税务主管当局提出预约定价安排申请的情况；
- 预约定价安排涉及的关联方最近3至5个年度生产经营情况及关联交易情况；
- 是否涉及国际重复征税及其说明。

A. Pre-filing Meeting

An enterprise with the intention to apply for an APA should submit a written application for pre-filing meeting to the tax administration(s). The tax administration(s) may schedule one or several pre-filing meetings with the enterprise.

(1) For a unilateral APA, the enterprise shall submit a written application for pre-filing meeting in the form of *APA Pre-filing Meeting Application Letter* to the in-charge tax administration(s). The in-charge tax administration(s) may schedule one or several pre-filing meetings with the enterprise.

For a bilateral/multilateral APA, the enterprise shall submit a written application for pre-filing meeting in the form of *APA Pre-filing Meeting Application Letter* to both the State Taxation Administration (STA) and the in-charge tax administration(s). The STA may schedule one or several pre-filing meetings with the enterprise.

(2) During the pre-filing meeting stage, the enterprise shall provide brief information on the following aspects:

i. Tax years to be covered by the APA;

ii. Related parties and related party transactions to be covered by the APA;

iii. Organizational and management structure of the enterprise and the group it belongs to;

iv. Business operations and contemporaneous transfer pricing documentation of the enterprise for the most recent 3 to 5 years, etc.;

v. Functions performed and risks assumed by the related parties covered by the APA, including the allocation keys based used to allocate the functions and risks, such as facilities, personnel, expenses, assets involved, etc.;

vi. Market conditions, including industry developments and trends, competitive environment, etc.;

vii. Location specific advantages such as cost savings and market premium (if any);

viii. Proposed rollback years (if any);

ix. Any other relevant information.

For a bilateral/multilateral APA, the enterprise should also provide information on the following aspects:

i. Status of APA request to the competent tax authority(ies) of the other Contracting State(s) of the tax treaty(ies);

ii. Business operations of the related parties covered by the APA and their related party transactions for the most recent 3 to 5 years;

iii. Double taxation involved and relevant explanations (if any).

（3）预备会谈期间，企业应当按照税务机关的要求补充资料。

2. 谈签意向

税务机关和企业在预备会谈期间达成一致意见的，主管税务机关向企业送达同意其提交谈签意向的《税务事项通知书》。企业收到《税务事项通知书》后向税务机关提出谈签意向。

（1）企业申请单边预约定价安排的，应当向主管税务机关提交《预约定价安排谈签意向书》，并附送单边预约定价安排申请草案。

企业申请双边或者多边预约定价安排的，应当同时向国家税务总局和主管税务机关提交《预约定价安排谈签意向书》，并附送双边或者多边预约定价安排申请草案。

（2）单边预约定价安排申请草案应当包括以下内容：

- 预约定价安排的适用年度；
- 预约定价安排涉及的关联方及关联交易；
- 企业及其所属企业集团的组织结构和管理架构；
- 企业最近3至5个年度生产经营情况、财务会计报告、审计报告、同期资料等；
- 预约定价安排涉及各关联方功能和风险的说明，包括功能和风险划分所依据的机构、人员、费用、资产等；
- 预约定价安排使用的定价原则和计算方法，以及支持这一定价原则和计算方法的功能风险分析、可比性分析和假设条件等；
- 价值链或者供应链分析，以及对成本节约、市场溢价等地域特殊优势的考虑；
- 市场情况的说明，包括行业发展趋势和竞争环境等；
- 预约定价安排适用期间的年度经营规模、经营效益预测以及经营规划等；
- 预约定价安排是否追溯适用以前年度；
- 对预约定价安排有影响的境内、外行业相关法律、法规；

(3) During the pre-filing meeting stage, the enterprise shall submit additional information as requested by the tax administration(s).

B. Letter of Intent

Where the tax administrations and the enterprise reach an agreement during the pre-filing meeting stage, the in-charge tax administration(s) shall issue a *Notice on Tax Matters* to the enterprise to inform the latter to submit the intent for the APA. The enterprise shall submit the intent for the APA to the tax administrations upon receipt of the *Notice on Tax Matters*.

(1) For a unilateral APA, the enterprise shall submit the *APA Letter of Intent* to the in-charge tax administration(s), with the draft unilateral APA application package attached.

For a bilateral/multilateral APA, the enterprise shall submit the *APA Letter of Intent* to both the STA and the in-charge tax administration(s), with the draft bilateral/multilateral APA application package attached.

(2) The draft unilateral APA application package should include information on the following aspects:
   i. Tax years to be covered by the APA;
   ii. Related parties and related party transactions to be covered by the APA;
   iii. Organizational and management structure of the enterprise and the group it belongs to;
   iv. Business operations, financial and accounting reports, audit reports, and contemporaneous transfer pricing documentation of the enterprise for the most recent 3 to 5 years, etc.;
   v. Functions performed, risks assumed by the related parties covered by the APA, including the allocation keys used to allocate the functions, risks, such as facilities, personnel, expenses, assets involved, etc.;
   vi. Proposed pricing methodologies and calculation process in the APA, and the functional and risk analysis, comparability analysis and assumptions supporting the proposed pricing methodologies and calculation process;
   vii. Value chain analysis or supply chain analysis, taking into account of location specific advantages such as cost savings and market premium, etc.;
   viii. Market conditions, including industry developments and trends, and competitive environment, etc.;
   ix. Annual scale of operation, profit and loss forecasts and business plans for the years to be covered by the APA;
   x. Proposed rollback years (if any);
   xi. The relevant industry laws and regulations in and outside China that have implications for the APA;

- 企业关于不存在下述第（3）项所列举情形的说明；
- 其他需要说明的情况。

双边或者多边预约定价安排申请草案还应当包括：

- 向税收协定缔约对方税务主管当局提出预约定价安排申请的情况；
- 预约定价安排涉及的关联方最近3至5个年度生产经营情况及关联交易情况；
- 是否涉及国际重复征税及其说明。

（3）有下列情形之一的，税务机关可以拒绝企业提交谈签意向：

- 税务机关已经对企业实施特别纳税调整立案调查或者其他涉税案件调查，且尚未结案的；
- 未按照有关规定填报年度关联业务往来报告表；
- 未按照有关规定准备、保存和提供同期资料；
- 预备会谈阶段税务机关和企业无法达成一致意见。

3. 分析评估

企业提交谈签意向后，税务机关应当分析预约定价安排申请草案内容，评估其是否符合独立交易原则。根据分析评估的具体情况可以要求企业补充提供有关资料。

税务机关可以从以下方面进行分析评估：

（1）功能和风险状况。分析评估企业与其关联方之间在供货、生产、运输、销售等各环节以及在研究、开发无形资产等方面各自做出的贡献、执行的功能以及在存货、信贷、外汇、市场等方面承担的风险。

（2）可比交易信息。分析评估企业提供的可比交易信息，对存在的实质性差异进行调整。

xii. Explanation that none of the circumstances listed in Clause (3) of this Article applies to the enterprise;

xiii. Any other relevant information.

The draft bilateral/multilateral APA application package should also include information on the following aspects:

i. Status of the APA request to the competent tax authority(ies) of the other Contracting State(s) of the tax treaty(ies);

ii. Business operations of the related parties covered by the APA and their related party transactions for the most recent 3 to 5 years;

iii. Double taxation involved and relevant explanations (if any).

(3) Tax administration(s) may disallow the enterprise to submit the intent for an APA if one or more of the following circumstances is present:

i. The enterprise is under open special tax adjustment investigation or other tax investigations;

ii. The enterprise fails to file the annual reporting forms for related party dealings of enterprises pursuant to the relevant regulations and requirements;

iii. The enterprise fails to prepare, keep and provide the contemporaneous transfer pricing documentation pursuant to the relevant regulations and requirements;

iv. No agreement is reached between the tax administration(s) and the enterprise during the pre-filing meeting stage.

C. Analysis and Evaluation

After receiving the intent for an APA from the enterprise, tax administration(s) shall analyse the draft APA application package and evaluate whether the proposed pricing methodologies and calculation process are in line with the arm's length principle. The tax administration(s) may request additional information based on the findings from their analysis and evaluation.

The analysis and evaluation may cover the following aspects:

(1) Functional and risk profile. Tax administrations(s) will analyse and evaluate functions performed and contribution made with respect to supply, production, logistics, sales, and research and development of intangibles, etc., as well as risks such as inventory risk, credit risk, foreign exchange risk and market risk assumed by the enterprise and its related parties respectively.

(2) Comparability analysis. Tax administration(s) will analyse and evaluate comparable information

（3）关联交易数据。分析评估预约定价安排涉及的关联交易的收入、成本、费用和利润是否单独核算或者按照合理比例划分。

（4）定价原则和计算方法。分析评估企业在预约定价安排中采用的定价原则和计算方法。如申请追溯适用以前年度的，应当作出说明。

（5）价值链分析和贡献分析。评估企业对价值链或者供应链的分析是否完整、清晰，是否充分考虑成本节约、市场溢价等地域特殊优势，是否充分考虑本地企业对价值创造的贡献等。

（6）交易价格或者利润水平。根据上述分析评估结果，确定符合独立交易原则的价格或者利润水平。

（7）假设条件。分析评估影响行业利润水平和企业生产经营的因素及程度，合理确定预约定价安排适用的假设条件。

分析评估阶段，税务机关可以与企业就预约定价安排申请草案进行讨论。税务机关可以进行功能和风险实地访谈。

4. 正式申请

税务机关认为预约定价安排申请草案不符合独立交易原则的，企业应当与税务机关协商，并进行调整；税务机关认为预约定价安排申请草案符合独立交易原则的，主管税务机关向企业送达同意其提交正式申请的《税务事项通知书》，企业收到通知后，可以向税务机关提交《预约定价安排正式申请书》，并附送预约定价安排正式申请报告。

（1）企业申请单边预约定价安排的，应当向主管税务机关提交上述资料。

企业申请双边或者多边预约定价安排的，应当同时向国家税务总局和主管税务机关提交上述资料，并在税收协定规定期限内，向国家税务总局书面提交《启动特别纳税调整相互协商程序申请表》。国家税务总局决定启动相互协商程序的，应当书面通知省税务机关，并告

provided by the enterprise, and make adjustment for substantial comparability differences.

(3) Related party transaction. Tax administration(s) will analyse and evaluate whether the revenue, cost, expenses and profits associated with the related party transactions cover by the APA are separately accounted for or determined based on reasonable allocation keys.

(4) Pricing methodologies and calculation process. Tax administration(s) will analyse and evaluate the proposed pricing methodologies and calculation process in the APA. Additional statement and explanation should be provided if an APA rollback is proposed.

(5) Value chain analysis and contribution analysis. Tax administration(s) will analyse and evaluate whether the value chain analysis or contribution analysis is complete and clear and whether due consideration is given to location specific advantages such as cost savings and market premium as well as to the contributions to the value creation made by the local enterprise.

(6) Transaction price or profit level. Tax administration(s) will determine the arm's length transaction price or profit level based on the findings from the analysis and evaluation on the aforementioned aspects.

(7) Assumptions. Tax administration(s) will analyse and evaluate the factors influencing the enterprise's profitability and business operation and the extent of the influence. Appropriate assumptions applied to the APA shall be established accordingly.

During the analysis and evaluation stage, tax administration(s) may discuss with the enterprise about the draft APA application package and conduct on-site functional interviews.

D. Formal Application

Where the proposal in the draft APA application package is not in line with the arm's length principle, the enterprise shall consult with the tax administration(s) and make adjustments accordingly. Where the proposal in the draft APA application package is in line with the arm's length principle, the in-charge tax administration(s) will issue the *Notice on Tax Matters* to notify the enterprise to submit the formal application for the APA. Upon receiving the notice, the enterprise shall submit the *APA Formal Application Letter* to the tax administration(s), with the formal APA application packaged attached.

(1) For a unilateral APA, the enterprise shall submit the aforementioned information and documents to the in-charge tax administration(s). For a bilateral/multilateral APA, the enterprise shall submit the aforementioned information and documents to both the STA and the in-charge tax administration(s)

知税收协定缔约对方税务主管当局。主管税务机关应当在收到书面通知后15个工作日内,向企业送达启动相互协商程序的《税务事项通知书》。

(2)有下列情形之一的,税务机关可以拒绝企业提交正式申请:

- 预约定价安排申请草案拟采用的定价原则和计算方法不合理,且企业拒绝协商调整;
- 企业拒不提供有关资料或者提供的资料不符合税务机关要求,且不按时补正或者更正;
- 企业拒不配合税务机关进行功能和风险实地访谈;
- 其他不适合谈签预约定价安排的情况。

5. 协商签署

税务机关应当在分析评估的基础上形成协商方案,并据此开展协商工作。

(1)主管税务机关与企业开展单边预约定价安排协商,协商达成一致的,拟定单边预约定价安排文本。

国家税务总局与税收协定缔约对方税务主管当局开展双边或者多边预约定价安排协商,协商达成一致的,拟定双边或者多边预约定价安排文本。

(2)预约定价安排文本可以包括以下内容:

- 企业及其关联方名称、地址等基本信息;
- 预约定价安排涉及的关联交易及适用年度;
- 预约定价安排选用的定价原则和计算方法,以及可比价格或者可比利润水平等;
- 与转让定价方法运用和计算基础相关的术语定义;
- 假设条件及假设条件变动通知义务;
- 企业年度报告义务;
- 预约定价安排的效力;
- 预约定价安排的续签;
- 预约定价安排的生效、修订和终止;

and simultaneously apply for the Mutual Agreement Procedure (MAP) process pursuant to the relevant regulations and requirements.

(2) Tax administration(s) may disallow the enterprise to submit the formal application for an APA if one or more of the following circumstances is present:

i. The proposed pricing methodologies and calculation process in the draft APA application package is found to be inappropriate and the enterprise refuses to consult with tax administration(s) and make adjustments;

ii. The enterprise fails to provide relevant information or provide additional and/or correct information despite the information originally provided has not met the requirements of the tax administration(s);

iii. The enterprise fails to cooperate with tax administration's request to conduct on-site functional interviews;

iv. Any other circumstances warranting the discontinuance of the APA process.

E. Negotiation and Signing

Tax administration(s) will form position on an APA based on the findings from the analysis and evaluation and conduct negotiation accordingly.

(1) For a unilateral APA, where an agreement is reached between the in-charge tax administration(s) and the enterprise, a unilateral APA agreement will be prepared.

For a bilateral/multilateral APA, where an agreement is reached between the STA and the competent authority(ies) of other contracting state(s) of the tax treaty(ies), a bilateral/multilateral APA agreement will be prepared.

(2) An APA agreement may include the following elements:

i. Basic information such as names and addresses of the enterprise and its related parties;

ii. Related party transactions and years covered by the APA;

iii. Selected pricing methodologies and calculation process, comparable prices or profit levels, etc.;

iv. Terms and definitions related to applied transfer pricing methodologies and calculation basis;

v. Assumptions and obligation to notify changes to the assumptions;

vi. Obligation to submit annual APA implementation report;

vii. Binding effect of the APA;

viii. Renewal of the APA;

ix. Validity, amendment and termination of the APA;

- 争议的解决；

- 文件资料等信息的保密义务；

- 单边预约定价安排的信息交换；

- 附则。

（3）主管税务机关与企业就单边预约定价安排文本达成一致后，双方的法定代表人或者法定代表人授权的代表签署单边预约定价安排。

国家税务总局与税收协定缔约对方税务主管当局就双边或者多边预约定价安排文本达成一致后，双方或者多方税务主管当局授权的代表签署双边或者多边预约定价安排。国家税务总局应当将预约定价安排转发主管税务机关。主管税务机关应当向企业送达《税务事项通知书》，附送预约定价安排，并做好执行工作。

（4）预约定价安排涉及适用年度或者追溯年度补（退）税款的，税务机关应当按照纳税年度计算应补征或者退还的税款，并向企业送达《预约定价安排补（退）税款通知书》。

6. 监控执行

税务机关应当监控预约定价安排的执行情况。

（1）预约定价安排执行期间，企业应当完整保存与预约定价安排有关的文件和资料，包括账簿和有关记录等，不得丢失、销毁和转移。

企业应当在纳税年度终了后6个月内，向主管税务机关报送执行预约定价安排情况的纸质版和电子版年度报告，主管税务机关将电子版年度报告报送国家税务总局；涉及双边或者多边预约定价安排的，企业应当向主管税务机关报送执行预约定价安排情况的纸质版和电子版年度报告，同时将电子版年度报告报送国家税务总局。

年度报告应当说明报告期内企业经营情况以及执行预约定价安排的情况。需要修订、终止预约定价安排，或者有未决问题或者预计将要发生问题的，应当作出说明。

x. Dispute resolution;

xi. Confidentiality of information and documents pertaining to the APA;

xii. Exchange of information on unilateral APAs;

xiii. Appendices.

(3) Where a unilateral APA agreement is reached between the in-charge tax administration(s) and the enterprise, legal representatives or representatives authorized by the legal representatives of the two parties shall sign the unilateral APA agreement.

Where a bilateral/multilateral APA agreement is reached between the STA and the competent authority(ies) of other contracting state(s) of the tax treaty(ies), authorized representatives of all the parties shall sign the bilateral/multilateral APA agreement. The STA shall forward a copy of the agreement to the in-charge tax administration(s). The in-charge tax administration(s) shall issue the *Notice on Tax Matters* with the copy of the agreement attached to the enterprise and ensure the implementation of the APA.

(4) Where an APA involves additional tax payments or tax refunds for the prospective years or rollback years, tax administration(s) shall calculate the amount of tax payable or tax refundable on a tax year-by-tax year basis and issue the *Notice on APA Tax Payable/Refundable.*

F. Implementation and Monitoring

Tax administration(s) shall monitor the implementation of APA.

(1) During the APA covered period, the enterprise shall keep the relevant information and documents (including accounting records and other relevant records) intact and shall not lose, destroy or remove such information and documents.

The enterprise shall file the annual APA implementation report in both hard copy and electronic copy with the in-charge tax administration(s) within 6 months of the end of each tax year. The in-charge tax administration(s) shall forward the electronic copy to the STA. For a bilateral/multilateral APA, the enterprise shall file the annual APA implementation report in both hard copy and electronic copy with the in-charge tax administration(s) and simultaneously file the electronic copy with the STA.

The annual APA implementation report shall document the enterprise's business operations and implementation of the APA during the reporting period. The enterprise shall also explain in the annual APA implementation report if there is a need to amend or terminate the APA, or if there are any unsettled issues or foreseeable issues.

（2）预约定价安排执行期间，主管税务机关应当每年监控企业执行预约定价安排的情况。监控内容主要包括：企业是否遵守预约定价安排条款及要求；年度报告是否反映企业的实际经营情况；预约定价安排所描述的假设条件是否仍然有效等。

（3）预约定价安排执行期间，企业发生影响预约定价安排的实质性变化，应当在发生变化之日起30日内书面报告主管税务机关，详细说明该变化对执行预约定价安排的影响，并附送相关资料。由于非主观原因而无法按期报告的，可以延期报告，但延长期限不得超过30日。

税务机关应当在收到企业书面报告后，分析企业实质性变化情况，根据实质性变化对预约定价安排的影响程度，修订或者终止预约定价安排。签署的预约定价安排终止执行的，税务机关可以和企业按照64号公告规定的程序和要求，重新谈签预约定价安排。

（三）追溯调整

企业以前年度的关联交易与预约定价安排适用年度相同或者类似的，经企业申请，税务机关可以将预约定价安排确定的定价原则和计算方法追溯适用于以前年度该关联交易的评估和调整。追溯期最长为10年。

预约定价安排的谈签不影响税务机关对企业不适用预约定价安排的年度及关联交易的特别纳税调查调整和监控管理。

经预备会谈与税务机关达成一致意见，已向税务机关提交《预约定价安排谈签意向书》，并申请预约定价安排追溯适用以前年度的企业，或者已向税务机关提交《预约定价安排续签申请书》的企业，可以暂不作为特别纳税调整的调查对象。预约定价安排未涉及的年度和关联交易除外。

(2) During the APA covered period, the in-charge tax administration(s) shall monitor the enterprise's implementation of the APA on a yearly basis. Major areas for monitoring include: whether the enterprise complies with the terms and conditions in the APA; whether the information provided in the annual APA implementation report reflects the actual operation results of the enterprise; whether the assumptions specified in the APA are still valid, etc.

(3) During the APA covered period, where there are substantial changes to the enterprise which may have an impact on the APA, the enterprise shall file a written report on substantial changes with the in-charge tax administration(s) within 30 days. The report should explain in detail the impact of the changes, with relevant supporting information and documents attached. If the enterprise is forced to delay the reporting due to circumstances beyond its control, an up to 30 days extension can be applied.

Upon receiving written report from the enterprise, tax administration(s) shall analyze to what extent the substantial changes have impacted the APA. Tax administration(s) may amend or terminate the APA depending on the extent of the impact. If the existing APA is terminated, tax administration(s) and the enterprise may start the APA process for the purpose of concluding a new APA pursuant to the relevant provisions and requirements of Public Notice No.64.

3. Rollback

Where the related party transactions in prior years are the same as or similar to those covered by the APA, per the enterprise's request, the tax administration(s) may apply the agreed pricing methodologies and calculation process specified in the APA to such related party transactions. The maximum rollback period is 10 years.

The conclusion of an APA does not preclude the enterprise from special tax adjustment investigation on related party transactions or years not covered by the APA.

Enterprises which have reached agreement in the pre-filing meeting with the tax authorities and submitted the *APA Letter of Intent* and applied for retroactive application of the APA, or enterprises which have submitted the *APA Renewal Application*, can be temporarily exempted from special tax audit. This exemption does not apply to the period and the related transactions which are not covered under the APA.

（四）续　签

1. 预约定价安排执行期满后自动失效。企业申请续签的，应当在预约定价安排执行期满之日前90日内向税务机关提出续签申请，报送《预约定价安排续签申请书》，并提供执行现行预约定价安排情况的报告，现行预约定价安排所述事实和经营环境是否发生实质性变化的说明材料以及续签预约定价安排年度的预测情况等相关资料。

2. 预约定价安排采用四分位法确定价格或者利润水平，在预约定价安排执行期间，如果企业当年实际经营结果在四分位区间之外，税务机关可以将实际经营结果调整到四分位区间中位值。预约定价安排执行期满，企业各年度经营结果的加权平均值低于区间中位值，且未调整至中位值的，税务机关不再受理续签申请。

双边或者多边预约定价安排执行期间存在上述问题的，主管税务机关应当及时将有关情况层报国家税务总局。

（五）暂停或终止

1. 在预约定价安排签署前，税务机关和企业均可暂停、终止预约定价安排程序。税务机关发现企业或者其关联方故意不提供与谈签预约定价安排有关的必要资料，或者提供虚假、不完整资料，或者存在其他不配合的情形，使预约定价安排难以达成一致的，可以暂停、终止预约定价安排程序。涉及双边或者多边预约定价安排的，经税收协定缔约各方税务主管当局协商，可以暂停、终止预约定价安排程序。税务机关暂停、终止预约定价安排程序的，应当向企业送达《税务事项通知书》，并说明原因；企业暂停、终止预约定价安排程序的，应当向税务机关提交书面说明。

2. 预约定价安排执行期间，主管税务机关与企业发生分歧的，双方应当进行协商。协商不能解决的，可以报上一级税务机关协调；涉及双边或者多边预约定价安排的，必须层

4. Renewal

(1) An APA automatically becomes invalid upon its expiration. The enterprise may apply for a renewal by filing an *APA Renewal Application* with the tax administration(s) within 90 days prior to the expiration of the existing APA. The enterprise shall also provide relevant supporting information and documents including annual APA implementation reports for the existing APA, documents explaining whether there have been any substantial changes to the facts and operating environment specified in the exiting APA, and forecast for the years to be covered by the APA renewal, etc.

(2) For an APA with a target price/profit within an interquartile range, if the enterprise's actual operating price/profit falls outside the interquartile range for any year during the APA covered period, tax administration(s) shall adjust the actual operating result to the median for the year. Upon expiration of the APA, if the calculated weighted average operating price/profit of the enterprise for the APA covered period falls below the median of the agreed range and is not adjusted to the median, tax administration(s) will not accept the enterprise's APA renewal application.

Where a bilateral/multilateral APA is involved, the in-charge tax administration(s) shall report the aforementioned issues to the STA in a timely manner.

5. Termination or Cancellation

(1) Either the tax administration(s) or the enterprise can suspend or terminate an APA process at any point of time before the conclusion of the APA. If the enterprise is found to have purposefully withheld relevant information, or provided false or incomplete information, or been uncooperative in other matters rendering the conclusion of the APA impossible, the tax administration(s) may suspend or terminate the APA process. For a bilateral/multilateral APA, the APA process may be suspended or terminated after consultation between the competent authorities involved. Where the tax administration(s) initiate the suspension or termination of the APA process, the tax administration(s) shall issue a *Notice on Tax Matters* to notify the enterprise of the decision and underlying reasons. Where the enterprise initiates the suspension or termination of the APA process, the enterprise shall submit a written explanation to the tax administration(s).

(2) In case any dispute arises during the implementation of an APA, the in-charge tax administration(s) and the enterprise shall endeavor to resolve the disputes through negotiations. Where the disputes remain unresolved after negotiations, the in-charge tax administration can report the disputes to the

报国家税务总局协调。对上一级税务机关或者国家税务总局的决定，下一级税务机关应当予以执行。企业仍不能接受的，可以终止预约定价安排的执行。

3. 没有按照规定的权限和程序签署预约定价安排，或者税务机关发现企业隐瞒事实的，应当认定预约定价安排自始无效，并向企业送达《税务事项通知书》，说明原因；发现企业拒不执行预约定价安排或者存在违反预约定价安排的其他情况，可以视情况进行处理，直至终止预约定价安排。

（六）涉及多个税务机关的情况

1. 预约定价安排同时涉及两个或者两个以上省、自治区、直辖市和计划单列市税务机关的，由国家税务总局统一组织协调。

企业申请上述单边预约定价安排的，应当同时向国家税务总局及其指定的税务机关提出谈签预约定价安排的相关申请。国家税务总局可以与企业统一签署单边预约定价安排，或者指定税务机关与企业统一签署单边预约定价安排，也可以由各主管税务机关与企业分别签署单边预约定价安排。

2. 单边预约定价安排涉及一个省、自治区、直辖市和计划单列市内两个或者两个以上主管税务机关的，由省、自治区、直辖市和计划单列市相应税务机关统一组织协调。

tax administration(s) at the higher level for mediation. Disputes that involve a bilateral/multilateral APA shall be reported to the STA for mediation. Decisions made by the tax administration(s) at the higher level or the STA shall be enforced by the in-charge tax administration(s). The APA may be terminated if the enterprise still finds the decisions unacceptable.

(3) Where the conclusion of an APA is found to be resulting from an APA process inconsistent with the relevant regulations and requirements or the fact that the enterprise has withheld information, the tax administration(s) will annul the APA and issue the *Notice on Tax Matters* to notify the enterprise of the decision and the underlying reasons. Where the enterprise is found to fail to implement an APA or violate the terms and conditions of an APA in other manners, the tax administration(s) may, depending on the circumstances, take necessary measures including terminating the APA to address the incompliance.

6. Particular Situations Referred to Multiple Tax Authorities

(1) Where an APA involves two or more provinces, autonomous regions, municipalities directly under the central government or cities specifically designated in the state plan, the APA process shall be organized and coordinated by the STA.

The enterprise applying for a unilateral APA that falls under one of the aforementioned categories shall submit the application to both the STA and the tax administration(s) designated by the STA. The STA may sign the unilateral APA with the enterprise by itself or authorize the designated tax administration(s) to sign the unilateral APA with the enterprise. Alternatively the STA may arrange for each relevant in-charge tax administration to sign the unilateral APA with the enterprise respectively.

(2) Where a unilateral APA involves two or more in-charge tax administrations within the same province, autonomous region, municipality directly under the central government or city specifically designated in the state plan , the APA process shall be organized and coordinated by the tax administration(s) at the level of the province, autonomous region, municipality directly under the central government or city specifically designated in the state plan.

四、单边预约定价安排简易程序操作规范

（一）申请及适用年度

1. 申请资格

企业在主管税务机关向其送达受理申请的《税务事项通知书》之日所属纳税年度前3个年度，每年度发生的关联交易金额在4000万元人民币以上，且符合下列条件之一的，可以申请适用单边预约定价安排简易程序：

（1）已向主管税务机关提供拟提交申请所属年度前3个纳税年度的、符合《国家税务总局关于完善关联申报和同期资料管理有关事项的公告》（国家税务总局公告2016年第42号）规定的同期资料；

（2）自企业提交申请之日所属纳税年度前10个年度内，曾执行预约定价安排，且执行结果符合安排要求的；

（3）自企业提交申请之日所属纳税年度前10个年度内，曾受到税务机关特别纳税调查调整且结案的。

2. 适用年度

简易程序适用于主管税务机关向企业送达受理其申请的《税务事项通知书》之日所属纳税年度起3至5个年度的关联交易。

（二）操作流程

如图4-1所示，简易程序包括申请评估、协商签署和监控执行3个阶段。

IV The Simplified Procedure for UAPA

1. Prerequisites and Tax Years to be Covered by UAPA Simplified Procedure

(1) Prerequisites

Access to the simplified procedure for UAPA is available to an enterprise where it meets any of the following conditions together with the annual related party transaction amount exceeding RMB 40 million for the three years prior to the year in which the *Notice on Tax Matters* is issued by the in-charge tax administration(s) notifying the acceptance of enterprise's application.

> i. For the three years prior to the year in which the enterprise would submit the application, the transfer pricing documentation which complies with the requirements of *Public Notice on Matters Regarding Refining the Filling of Related Party Transactions and Administration of Contemporaneous Transfer Pricing Documentation* (Public Notice of the State Taxation Administration〔2016〕No. 42) have been submitted.
>
> ii. The enterprise has once implemented an APA in accordance with the requirements of APA agreement within 10 years prior to the year in which the enterprise would submit the application.
>
> iii. The enterprise was once under special tax adjustment investigation and the investigation has been concluded within 10 years prior to the year in which the enterprise would submit the application.

(2) Tax Years to be Covered by UAPA Simplified Procedure

The UAPA simplified procedure applies to related party transactions over a period of 3 to 5 consecutive years starting from the year during which the *Notice on Tax Matters* is issued by the in-charge tax administration(s) notifying the acceptance of enterprise's application.

2. The Process of UAPA Simplified Procedure

The process of UAPA simplified procedure involves the following three stages: application and evaluation, negotiation and signing, and implementation and monitoring (see Chart 4-1).

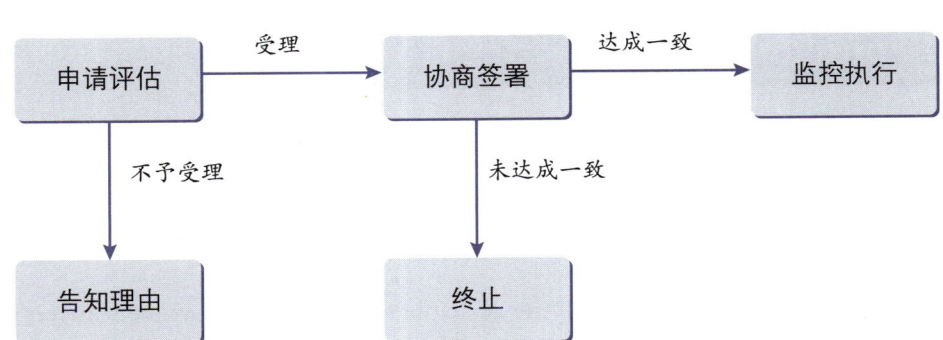

图4-1　单边预约定价安排简易程序操作流程

1. 申请评估

企业应当向主管税务机关提出适用简易程序的申请,主管税务机关分析评估后,决定是否受理。

(1)企业有申请意向的,应当向主管税务机关提交《单边预约定价安排适用简易程序申请书》,并附送申请报告。申请报告包括以下内容:

- 单边预约定价安排涉及的关联方及关联交易;
- 单边预约定价安排的适用年度;
- 单边预约定价安排是否追溯适用以前年度;
- 企业及其所属企业集团的组织结构和管理架构;
- 企业最近3至5个纳税年度生产经营情况、财务会计报告、审计报告、同期资料等;
- 单边预约定价安排涉及各关联方功能和风险的说明,包括功能和风险划分所依据的机构、人员、费用、资产等;
- 单边预约定价安排使用的定价原则和计算方法,可比价格或者可比利润水平,以及支持这一定价原则和计算方法的功能风险分析、可比性分析和假设条件等;
- 价值链或者供应链分析,以及对成本节约、市场溢价等地域特殊优势的考虑;

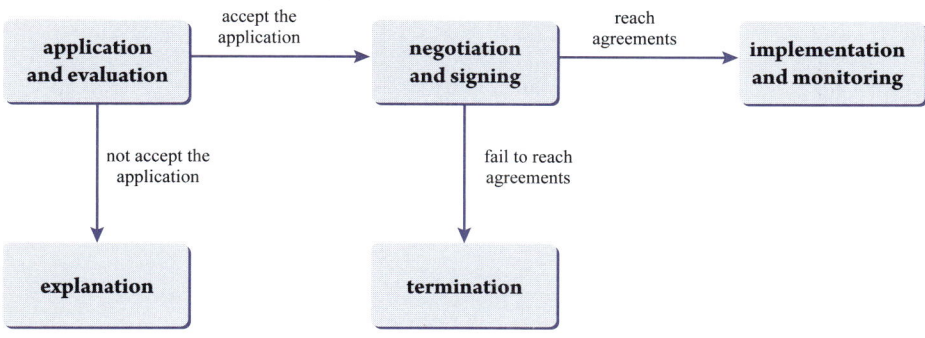

Chart 4-1 The Process of UAPA Simplified Procedure

A. Application and Evaluation

The enterprise should submit an application to the in-charge tax administration to apply for the simplified procedure for UAPA. The in-charge tax administration shall then decide whether to accept the application after evaluation.

(1) The enterprise with intention to apply to the simplified procedure should submit *Application Letter for UAPA to Apply to Simplified Procedure* to the in-charge tax administration, with the application report attached. The application report should include information on the following aspects:

i. Related parties and related party transactions to be covered by the UAPA;

ii. Tax years to be covered by the UAPA;

iii. Roll-back years (if any);

iv. Organizational and management structure of the enterprise and the group it belongs to;

v. Business operations, financial and accounting reports, audit reports, and contemporaneous transfer pricing documentation of the enterprise for the most recent 3-5 years;

vi. Functions performed, risks assumed by the related parties covered by the UAPA, including the allocation keys used to allocate the functions, risks, such as facilities, personnel, expenses, assets involved, etc.;

vii. Proposed pricing methodologies and calculation process in the UAPA, comparable prices or profit level, as well as the functional and risk analysis, comparability analysis and assumption supporting the proposed pricing methodology and calculation process;

viii. Value chain or supply chain analysis, taking into account of location specific advantages such as

- 市场情况的说明，包括行业发展趋势和竞争环境等；

- 单边预约定价安排适用期间的年度经营规模、经营效益预测以及经营规划等；

- 对单边预约定价安排有影响的境内、外行业相关法律、法规；

- 符合上述申请资格的有关情况；

- 其他需要说明的情况。

（2）有下列情形之一的，税务机关可以不予受理企业提交的申请：

- 税务机关已经对企业实施特别纳税调整立案调查或者其他涉税案件调查，且尚未结案；

- 未按照有关规定填报年度关联业务往来报告表，且不按时更正；

- 未按照有关规定准备、保存和提供同期资料；

- 未按照24号公告要求提供相关资料或者提供的资料不符合税务机关要求，且不按时补正或者更正；

- 拒不配合税务机关进行功能和风险实地访谈。

（3）主管税务机关收到企业的申请后，应当开展分析评估，进行功能和风险实地访谈，并于收到企业申请之日起90日内向企业送达《税务事项通知书》，告知其是否受理；不予受理的，说明理由。

2. 协商签署

主管税务机关受理企业申请后，应当与企业就其关联交易是否符合独立交易原则进行协商，并于向企业送达受理申请的《税务事项通知书》之日起6个月内协商完毕。协商期间，主管税务机关可以要求企业补充提交相关资料，企业补充提交资料时间不计入上述6个月内。

cost savings and market premium, etc.;

ix. Market conditions, including industry developments and trends, and competitive environment, etc.;

x. Annual scale of operation, profit and loss forecasts and business plan for the years to be covered by the UAPA;

xi. The relevant industry laws and regulations in and outside China that have implications for the UAPA;

xii. Relevant information that the enterprise meets above prerequisites to apply to simplified procedure;

xiii. Any other relevant information.

(2) Tax administration(s) may reject the application filed by the enterprise if one or more of the following circumstances is present:

i. The enterprise is under open special tax adjustment investigation or other tax investigations;

ii. The enterprise fails to file the annual reporting forms for related party dealings of enterprises pursuant to the relevant regulations and requirements, and doesn't make corrections on schedule;

iii. The enterprise fails to prepare keep and provide the contemporaneous transfer pricing documentation pursuant to the relevant regulations and requirements;

iv. The enterprise fails to provide information in accordance with the Public Notice No. 24 or provide additional and/or correct information despite the information originally provided has not met the requirements of the tax administration(s);

v. The enterprise fails to cooperate with tax administration's request to conduct on-site functional interviews.

(3) The in-charge tax administration(s) shall conduct analysis and evaluation as well as on-site functional interviews upon receiving the enterprise's application, and issue a *Notice on Tax Matters* to the enterprise within 90 days to inform the enterprise about whether the application is accepted. Explanations would be given if the application is not accepted.

B. Negotiation and Signing

After accepting the application submitted by the enterprise, the in-charge tax administration(s) shall negotiate with the enterprise on whether the proposed related transactions are in line with the arm's length principle.The negotiation shall be completed within 6 months after issuing the *Notice on Tax Matters* to the enterprise for accepting the application. During the negotiation, the in-charge tax administration(s) may request additional information, and the time taken for the enterprise to prepare such information is not

（1）主管税务机关与企业协商一致的，应当拟定单边预约定价安排文本。双方的法定代表人或法定代表人授权的代表签署单边预约定价安排。

（2）主管税务机关不能与企业协商一致的，应当向企业送达终止简易程序的《税务事项通知书》。企业可以按照64号公告的规定，重新申请单边预约定价安排。已提交过的资料，无须重复提交。

3. 监控执行

税务机关应当按照64号公告的要求，做好单边预约定价安排的监控执行工作。

单边预约定价安排执行期间，企业发生影响单边预约定价安排的实质性变化，导致终止执行的，可以按照24号公告规定，重新申请单边预约定价安排。

（三）其他事项

1. 同时涉及两个或者两个以上省、自治区、直辖市和计划单列市税务机关的单边预约定价安排，暂不适用简易程序。

2. 24号公告未做具体规定的其他单边预约定价安排事项，按64号公告的规定执行。

included in the above-mentioned 6 months.

(1) Where an agreement is reached between the in-charge tax administration(s) and the enterprise, a unilateral APA agreement will be prepared and legal representatives or representatives authorized by the legal representatives of the two parties shall sign the agreement.

(2) Where an agreement cannot be reached between the in-charge tax administration(s) and the enterprise, the in-charge tax administration(s) shall issue the *Notice on Tax Matters* to the enterprise to terminate the simplified procedure. The enterprise may re-apply for a unilateral APA in accordance the Public Notice No. 64, and the information that has already been provided before does not need to be submitted repeatedly.

C. Implementation and Monitoring

The in-charge tax administration(s) shall ensure the implementation and monitoring of the unilateral APA in accordance with the Public Notice No. 64.

During the unilateral APA covered period, where there are substantial changes to the enterprise which have impacts on and finally lead to the termination of, the unilateral APA, the enterprise may re-apply the unilateral APA in line with the Public Notice No. 24.

3. Other Issues

(1) Where an APA involves two or more provinces, autonomous regions, municipalities directly under the central government or cities specifically designated in the state plan, the simplified procedure is temporarily not applicable.

(2) Other matters regarding a unilateral APA that are not specified in the Public Notice No. 24 shall follow the regulations of Public Notice No. 64.

五、预约定价安排中纳税人权利保障

（一）纳税人信息保密

1. 税务机关与企业在预约定价安排谈签过程中取得的所有信息资料，双方均负有保密义务。除依法应当向有关部门提供信息的情况外，未经纳税人同意，税务机关不得以任何方式泄露预约定价安排相关信息。

2. 除涉及国家安全的信息以外，国家税务总局可以按照对外缔结的国际公约、协定、协议等有关规定，与其他国家（地区）税务主管当局就2016年4月1日以后签署的单边预约定价安排文本实施信息交换。企业应当在签署单边预约定价安排时提供其最终控股公司、上一级直接控股公司及单边预约定价安排涉及的境外关联方所在国家（地区）的名单。

（二）纳税人缔约自由

在预约定价安排签署前，税务机关和企业均可暂停、终止预约定价安排程序。

税务机关与企业不能达成预约定价安排的，税务机关在协商过程中所取得的有关企业的提议、推理、观念和判断等非事实性信息，不得用于对该预约定价安排涉及关联交易的特别纳税调查调整。

V Protection of Taxpayers' Rights

1. Confidentiality of Taxpayers' Information

(1) Both the tax administration(s) and the enterprise are legally bound to keep the information and documents obtained through the APA process confidential. Except for situations where the tax administration(s) are required by laws and regulations to share the information and documents with the relevant government agencies, the tax administration(s) are prohibited from disclosing the information and documents in any way without the consent of the enterprise.

(2) The STA may exchange information on unilateral APAs concluded after 1 April, 2016 with relevant competent authorities of other countries (regions) pursuant to the relevant international conventions, treaties, agreements between China and other countries (regions) unless the information concerns national security. The enterprise shall provide a list consisting of jurisdictions of its ultimate parent company, jurisdictions of its immediate parent company and jurisdictions of related party with whom it enters into a transaction covered by the APA to the tax administration(s) upon the conclusion of the APA.

2. Taxpayers' Freedom of Contract

Either the tax administration(s) or the enterprise can suspend or terminate an APA process at any point of time before the conclusion of the APA.

Where the tax administration(s) and the enterprise fail to conclude an APA, the tax administration(s) are refrained from using the nonfactual information such as proposals, inferences, views and positions obtained through the APA process in the special tax adjustment investigation on the related party transactions covered by the proposed APA.

六、预约定价安排统计数据

（一）预约定价安排年度分布

表6-1列示了2005—2020年（2005年1月1日至2020年12月31日，下同）16年间，中国每年签署的单边和双边预约定价安排（以下简称APA）数量。

表6-1　　　　　　　　APA分年度签署数量统计（2005—2020年）

年度	单边APA	双边APA	多边APA	合计
2005	13	1	0	14
2006	10	0	0	10
2007	7	3	0	10
2008	6	1	0	7
2009	5	7	0	12
2010	4	4	0	8
2011	8	4	0	12
2011（续签）	(4)	(0)	(0)	(4)
2012	3	9	0	12
2012（续签）	(1)	(6)	(0)	(7)
2013	11	8	0	19
2013（续签）	(0)	(4)	(0)	(4)
2014	3	6	0	9
2014（续签）	(1)	(0)	(0)	(1)
2015	6	6	0	12
2015（续签）	(0)	(2)	(0)	(2)
2016	8	6	0	14
2016（续签）	(0)	(2)	(0)	(2)
2017	3	5	0	8
2017（续签）	(0)	(3)	0	(3)

China Advance Pricing Arrangement Annual Report (2020)

VI APA Statistics

1. APAs Signed by Year

Exhibit 6-1 summarizes the number of unilateral and bilateral APAs that the Chinese tax authorities signed during each of the 2005 to 2020 calendar years.

Exhibit 6–1   APAs Signed by Year (2005–2020)

Year	Unilateral APAs	Bilateral APAs	Multilateral APAs	Total
2005	13	1	0	14
2006	10	0	0	10
2007	7	3	0	10
2008	6	1	0	7
2009	5	7	0	12
2010	4	4	0	8
2011	8	4	0	12
(Renewals in 2011)	(4)	(0)	(0)	(4)
2012	3	9	0	12
(Renewals in 2012)	(1)	(6)	(0)	(7)
2013	11	8	0	19
(Renewals in 2013)	(0)	(4)	(0)	(4)
2014	3	6	0	9
(Renewals in 2014)	(1)	(0)	(0)	(1)
2015	6	6	0	12
(Renewals in 2015)	(0)	(2)	(0)	(2)
2016	8	6	0	14
(Renewals in 2016)	(0)	(2)	(0)	(2)
2017	3	5	0	8
(Renewals in 2017)	(0)	(3)	(0)	(3)

续表

年度	单边APA	双边APA	多边APA	合计
2018	2	7	0	9
2018（续签）	（1）	（1）	（0）	（2）
2019	12	9	0	21
2019（续签）	（1）	（1）	（0）	（2）
2020	15	14	0	29
2020（续签）	（4）	（6）	（0）	（10）
合计	**116**	**90**	**0**	**206**

图6-1列示了2005—2020年单边APA和双边APA签署数量的对比。

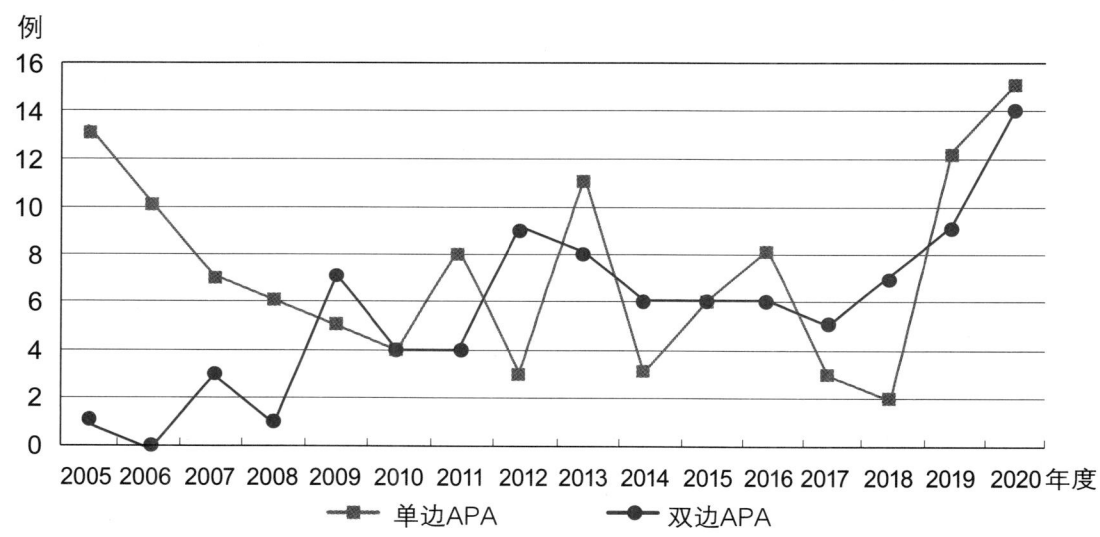

图6-1 APA签署数量统计（2005—2020年）

从表6-1和图6-1中可以看出，中国16年间共签署了116例单边APA、90例双边APA，分别占APA总数的56.31%和43.69%，目前中国尚未签署多边APA。2010—2020年，单边APA和双边APA的签署数量呈现波动性变化趋势。2020年，单边APA和双边APA工作稳步推进，签署数量共计29例。15例单边APA中11例为首轮签署，4例为续签；14例双边APA中8例为首轮签署，6例为续签。

(Continued)

Year	Unilateral APAs	Bilateral APAs	Multilateral APAs	Total
2018	2	7	0	9
(Renewals in 2018)	(1)	(1)	(0)	(2)
2019	12	9	0	21
(Renewals in 2019)	(1)	(1)	(0)	(2)
2020	15	14	0	29
(Renewals in 2020)	(4)	(6)	(0)	(10)
Total	116	90	0	206

The chart 6-1 compares the number of unilateral APAs and bilateral APAs signed from 2005 through 2020.

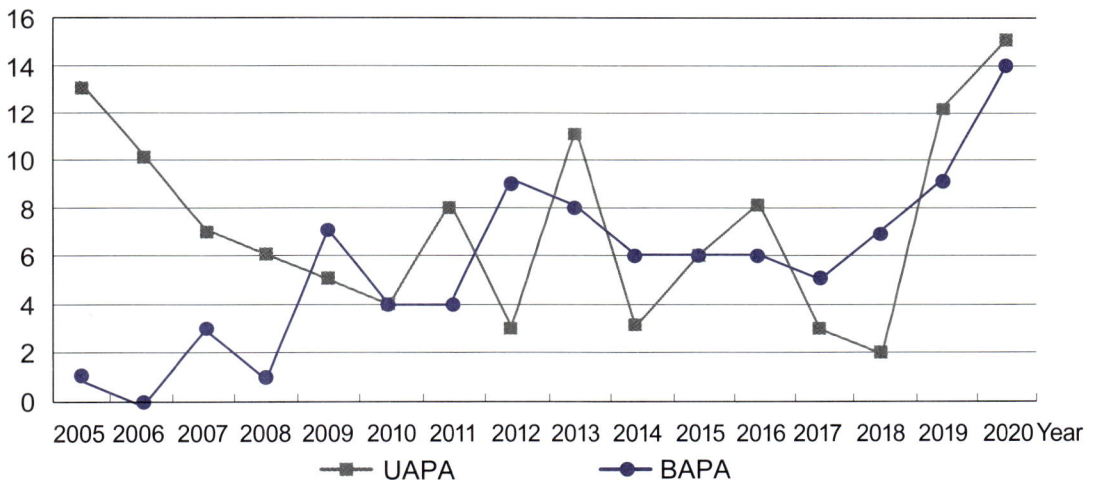

Chart 6-1 Number of APAs Signed (2005–2020)

As shown in the exhibit 6-1 and chart 6-1, China has signed 116 unilateral APAs and 90 bilateral APAs during this 15 year period, accounting for 56.31% and 43.69% of the total number of signed APAs in China respectively. So far China has not signed any multilateral APA. The number of APAs signed each year fluctuated from 2010 to 2020. Of the 14 bilateral APAs signed in 2020, 8 were signed for the first time and 6 were renewal. Of the 15 unilateral APAs signed in 2020, 11 were signed for the first time and another 4 were renewal. Altogether there were 29 APAs signed in 2020.

（二）预约定价安排谈签阶段分布

表6-2列示了2005—2020年中国预约定价安排分阶段统计数据。

表6-2　　　　　　　APA谈签阶段分布统计（2005—2020年）

APA所处阶段	单边	双边	合计
意向阶段	0	35	**35**
申请阶段	12	80	**92**
签署阶段	116	90	**206**

表6-2将预约定价安排谈签阶段划分为意向、申请和签署三个阶段[①]。这是根据64号公告相关规定做出的调整。

从各阶段单双边APA的数据对比来看，处于意向阶段和申请阶段的单边APA数量远小于双边APA数量。这一指标说明企业当前更愿意通过申请双边APA来获得税收确定性，同时避免或消除国际双重征税；另一方面也说明双边APA的受理和谈签工作量随着申请的增加而不断加大。

（三）预约定价安排交易类型分布

表6-3列示了2005—2020年中国已签署的APA涉及的关联交易类型[②]。

[①] 意向阶段指税务机关接受企业谈签意向的阶段，申请阶段指税务机关接受企业正式申请的阶段，签署阶段指税务机关与企业签署单边、双边预约定价安排的阶段。
[②] 由于部分预约定价安排涉及多种类型的关联交易，因此造成关联交易的合计数量要多于预约定价安排数量。

China Advance Pricing Arrangement Annual Report (2020)

2. APAs by Phase

Exhibit 6-2 provides statistics of APAs by phase as of December 31, 2020.

Exhibit 6-2   APAs by Phase (2005–2020)

Phases	Unilateral	Bilateral	Total
Intent	0	35	**35**
Application	12	80	**92**
Signing	116	90	**206**

According to *Public Notice on Matters Regarding Enhancing the Administration of Advance Pricing Arrangements* (Public Notice of the State Taxation Administration〔2016〕No. 64), Exhibit 6-2 adjusts and divides APA program into three phases, which are intent, application and signing[①].

As can be seen clearly in Exhibit 6-2, there are more bilateral APAs than unilateral APAs in intent phase and application phase. The above figures suggest that more and more enterprises prefer to apply for bilateral APA to gain certainty and avoid double taxation. They also demonstrate that the workload of Chinese tax administration in dealing with bilateral APA issues will dramatically increase as the growth of APA applications.

3. APAs by Transaction Type

Exhibit 6-3 below illustrates the types of transactions[②] involved in the concluded APAs as of December 31, 2020.

---

① The intent refers to the phase that the tax administrations accept the letter of intent of taxpayers; application refers to the phase that the tax administrations accept the formal application; signing refers the phase that the tax administrations are going to sign unilateral or bilateral APA with the taxpayers.

② As some APAs involve multiple transaction types, the total number of related party transactions is greater than the number of APAs.

表6-3　已签署APA涉及关联交易类型统计（2005—2020年）

关联交易类型	数量	比重
有形资产使用权或者所有权转让	172	58.11%
无形资产使用权或者所有权转让	55	18.58%
劳务交易	69	23.31%
资金融通	0	0
金融资产转让	0	0
合　计	296	100%

从表6-3可以看出，中国APA涉及的关联交易类型主要是有形资产使用权或者所有权的转让。已签署APA所涉及的有形资产使用权或者所有权转让占全部关联交易类型的58.11%；涉及无形资产使用权或者所有权转让，以及劳务交易的比重分别为18.58%和23.31%。随着中国第三产业的发展，越来越多的服务业企业将申请APA，未来APA也将更多地涉及无形资产所有权和使用权的转让、劳务交易、资金融通和金融资产转让。

（四）双边预约定价安排区域分布

2005—2020年，中国与亚洲国家（地区）签署了59例双边APA，与欧洲国家签署了19例双边APA，与北美洲国家签署了11例双边APA，与大洋洲国家签署了1例双边APA。双边APA的区域分布如图6-2所示。

China Advance Pricing Arrangement Annual Report (2020)

Exhibit 6-3   Concluded APAs by Transaction Type (2005–2020)

Transaction Type	Number of APAs	Percentage
Transfer of the right to use or ownership of tangible assets	172	58.11%
Transfer of the right to use or ownership of intangibles	55	18.58%
Services	69	23.31%
Financing	0	0
Transfer of financial assets	0	0
Total	296	100%

As shown in Exhibit 6-3, transfer of the right to use or ownership of tangible assets accounts for the largest portion of transactions covered by China's APA program. Of the concluded APAs, 58.11% involve transfer of the right to use or ownership of tangible assets, 18.58% involve transfer of the right to use or ownership of intangibles, and 23.31% involve services. As China's tertiary industry develops, an increasing number of service companies may decide to apply for APAs. Thus, more APAs may involve transactions related to transfer of the right to use or ownership of intangibles, services, financing and transfer of financial assets.

4. Bilateral APAs by Region

From 2005 to 2020, China has signed 59 bilateral APAs with Asian countries(regions), 19 with European countries,11 with North American countries and 1 with an Oceania country. The following chart displays the percentage of bilateral APAs accounted for by each of these regions (see Chart 6-2).

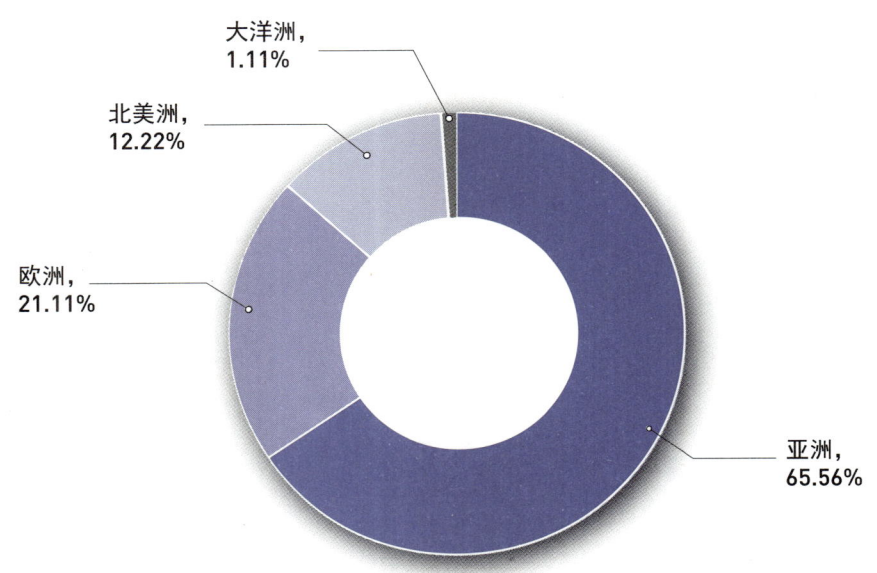

图6-2　双边预约定价安排区域分布（2005—2020年）

（五）预约定价安排完成时间

表6-4列示了2020年中国签署的单边APA和双边APA的完成时间。

表6-4　APA完成时间统计（2020年）

类型	从正式申请到达成安排所需时间				
	1年以内（含1年）	1～2年（含2年）	2～3年（含3年）	3年以上	合计
单边	13	0	2	0	15
双边	2	0	2	10	14

从表6-4可以看出，2020年中国签署的单边APA有13例在1年内完成，2例在2～3年完成，签署的双边APA中，2例在1年以内完成，2例在2～3年完成，10例耗时3年以上完成。

China Advance Pricing Arrangement Annual Report (2020)

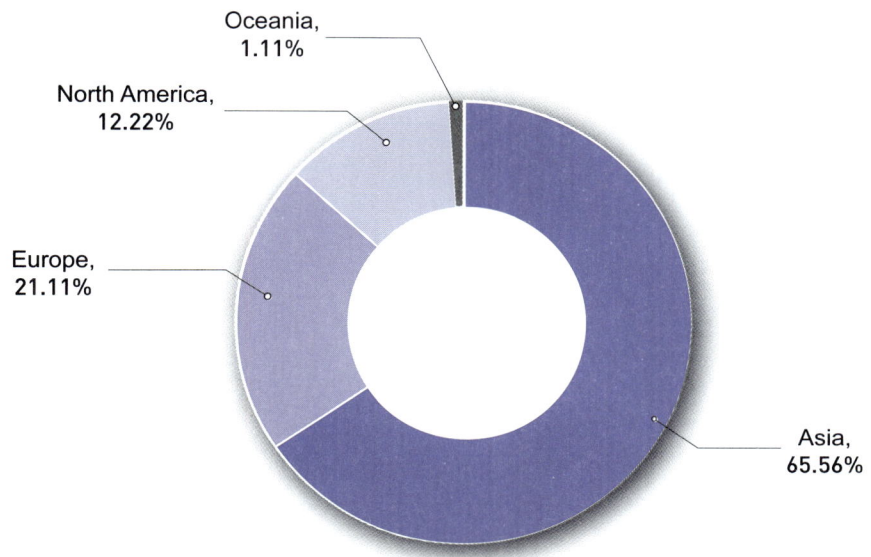

Chart 6-2 Bilateral APAs by Region (2005–2020)

5. APAs by Time Taken

Exhibit 6-4 illustrates the time taken to conclude unilateral and bilateral APAs signed by China in 2020.

Exhibit 6-4 APAs by Time Taken (2020)

Type	from Application to Conclusion				
	<1 year (including 1 year)	1–2 years (including 2 years)	2–3 years (including 3 years)	>3 years	Total
Unilateral	13	0	2	0	**15**
Bilateral	2	0	2	10	**14**

As shown in Exhibit 6-4, of the 15 unilateral APAs signed in 2020, 13 were concluded within 1 year and 2 were concluded in 2-3 years. Besides, of the 14 bilateral APAs signed in 2020, 2 were concluded within 1 year, 2 were concluded in 2-3 years while the remaining 10 took more than 3 years.

表6-5列示了2005—2020年中国签署的单边APA和双边APA的完成时间。

表6-5　　　　　　　APA完成时间统计（2005—2020年）

类型	从正式申请到达成安排所需时间				
	1年以内（含1年）	1～2年（含2年）	2～3年（含3年）	3年以上	合计
单边	66	37	9	4	**116**
双边	38	11	12	29	**90**

从表6-5可以看出，中国单边APA绝大部分在2年内完成，其中1年内完成的比例为56.9%，1～2年完成的比例为31.9%；2年以上完成的比例仅为11.2%。双边APA的完成时间通常比单边要长，但多数也在2年内完成，完成比例为54.44%，其中1年以内完成的比例为42.22%，1～2年完成的比例为12.22%；2～3年完成的比例和3年以上完成的比例分别13.33%和32.23%。

APA的完成时间取决于很多因素，如APA类型（单边、双边或多边）、APA涉及关联交易及有关问题的复杂程度、企业申请文本的质量、对方税务主管当局的审核速度（双边或多边APA），以及企业的配合程度（提供相关资料是否及时、完整）等。由于双边APA要根据税收协定、协议或者安排与其他国家（地区）税务主管当局启动相互协商程序，因此，相对于单边APA，达成双边APA所需的时间往往更长。

（六）预约定价安排使用的转让定价方法

图6-3列示了中国2005—2020年已签署的单边APA和双边APA所使用的转让定价方法[①]。

[①] 有的预约定价安排涉及两种或两种以上的关联交易，所使用的转让定价方法也可能涉及两种或两种以上。

Exhibit 6-5 illustrates the time taken for the unilateral and bilateral APAs to be signed by China from 2005 to 2020.

Exhibit 6-5   APAs by Time Taken (2005–2020)

Type	from Application to Conclusion				Total
	<1 year (including 1 year)	1–2 years (including 2 years)	2–3 years (including 3 years)	>3 years	
Unilateral	66	37	9	4	116
Bilateral	38	11	12	29	90

As shown in Exhibit 6-5, 56.9% of China's unilateral APAs were concluded within 1 year, 31.9% were concluded in 1 to 2 years while only 11.2% took more than 2 years. While bilateral APAs generally took more time, 42.22% were concluded within 1 year, 12.22% took 1 to 2 years, 13.33% took 2 to 3 years, and the remaining 32.23% were concluded in more than 3 years.

The time required to complete the entire APA process depends on many factors including the type of APA requested (i.e. unilateral, bilateral, or multilateral), the complexity of transactions involved, the quality of the documents provided by the taxpayer, the logistics of the review process performed by competent authorities. Bilateral APAs involve negotiations with relevant competent authorities through the MAP process and therefore more time is required to reach a consensus on them than that of unilateral APAs.

6. APAs by Transfer Pricing Method

The chart 6-3 shows the transfer pricing methods[①] applied in the unilateral and bilateral APAs signed from 2005 to 2020.

---

① Some APAs involve two or more types of transactions and multiple transfer pricing methods may be used.

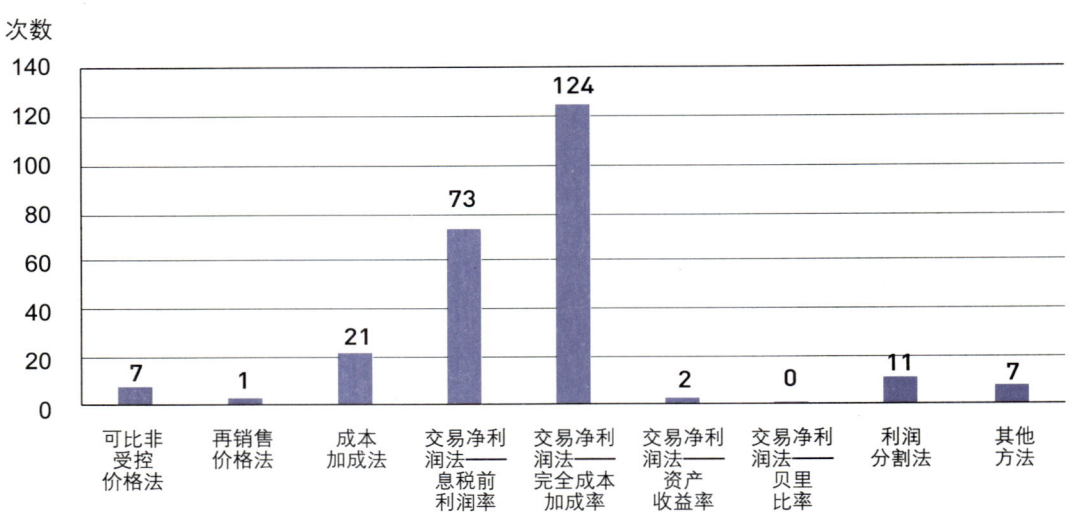

图6-3 已签署APA使用的转让定价方法（2005—2020年）

图6-3数据显示，交易净利润法是最常用的方法，使用199次，占全部方法的80.89%，主要采用的利润率指标是息税前利润率（73次）和完全成本加成率（124次）。同时，税务总局和各地主管税务局也积极尝试在预约定价安排中使用其他公平合理的转让定价方法，特别是在处理交易双方对价值创造都做出重要贡献的情况和存在市场溢价、成本节约等特殊地域优势的情况时。另一种较常使用的转让定价方法是成本加成法（21次）。可比非受控价格法、再销售价格法、利润分割法和其他方法较少使用，分别采用7次、1次、11次和7次。由于可比非受控价格法在使用过程中对产品和交易的可比性要求非常高，再销售价格法和利润分割法要求企业提供充足的交易及价格信息，导致这些方法在实际工作中被较少运用。中国税务机关希望申请APA的企业能够更好地配合税务人员的审核工作，提供充足的交易及价格信息，促进再销售价格法和利润分割法等转让定价方法的更多运用。

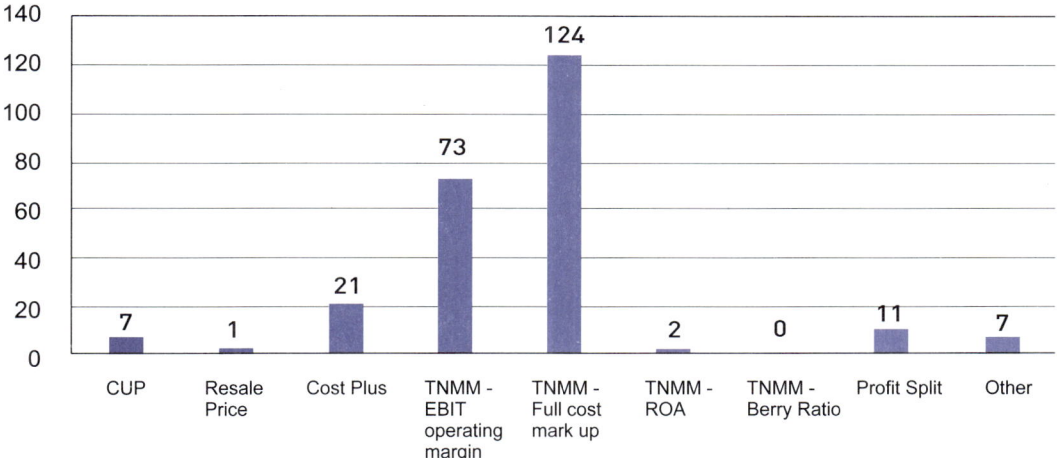

Chart 6-3 Transfer Pricing Methods Applied in APAs Signed (2005–2020)

The data indicates that the transactional net margin method (TNMM) is the most commonly used transfer pricing method, being used 199 times and accounting for 80.89% of all the applied transfer pricing methods. The most commonly used profit level indicators are the EBIT operating margin (used in 73 APAs) and the Full Cost Mark-up (used in 124 APAs). Meanwhile, the STA and local tax administrations have been exploring the use of other appropriate transfer pricing methods including profit split method especially in dealing with transactions where both transacted parties have made significant contributions to the value creation or location specific advantages such as market premium or cost savings have been present. The second most popular transfer pricing method is the cost plus method, being used in 21 of the concluded APAs. The other transfer pricing methods are applied less frequently. The comparable uncontrolled price(CUP) method is used in 7 cases, the resale price method in 1 case, the profit split method in 11 cases and other methods in the other 7 signed APAs. As the CUP method requires a very high standard of comparability for application and the resale price method and profit split method require a heavy amount of information regarding the transaction and pricing, these methods tend to be applied less frequently in practice. The Chinese tax authorities hope that enterprises will better cooperate with tax officers during the APA review and evaluation phase and provide sufficient information regarding transactions and prices so that the resale price method and the profit split method may be more frequently applied in the APA program.

(七)预约定价安排涉及的行业

表6-6列示了中国2005—2020年签署的APA所涉及的行业[①]。从表6-6可以看出,制造业的预约定价安排仍是已签署安排的主体,占总数的80.1%。

表6-6　　已签署APA所涉及行业统计(2005—2020年)

行　　业	数　量
制造业	165
租赁和商务服务业	8
批发和零售业	21
交通运输、仓储和邮政业	4
科学研究和技术服务业	2
信息传输、软件和信息技术服务业	3
电力、热力燃气及水生产和供应业	1
建筑业	1
餐饮业	1
合　　计	206

[①] 行业划分依据国家统计局公布的《国民经济行业分类》。对我国预约定价安排未涉及的行业类型,本表未予列示。

7. Industries Covered by Signed APAs

Exhibit 6-6 illustrates the industries covered by the unilateral and bilateral APAs signed by China from 2005 to 2020. 80.1% of the APAs signed from 2005 to 2020 still involve manufacturing industry.

Exhibit 6-6   Industries Covered for APAs Signed (2005–2020)

Industry Involved	Number
Manufacturing	165
Leasing and Commercial Services	8
Wholesale trade and retail	21
Transportation, warehousing, and postal services	4
Scientific and technical services	2
Information transmission, software and information technology services	3
Electricity, thermo, gas and water generation and supply	1
Construction	1
Catering	1
Total	**206**

七、预约定价安排申请联系人信息

单位	联系人	联系电话	联系地址
国家税务总局	田 川	010-63410887	北京市西城区菜园街1号院
国家税务总局北京市税务局	马晓雯	010-60907182	北京市东城区天坛东路甲72号
国家税务总局天津市税务局	王春娣	022-24465656	天津市河北区民主道16号
国家税务总局河北省税务局	马振宇	0311-88625325	河北省石家庄市平安南大街35号
国家税务总局山西省税务局	杨晋	0351-2387616	山西省太原市迎泽区水西门街31号
国家税务总局内蒙古自治区税务局	隋洪峰	0471-3309112	内蒙古自治区呼和浩特市金桥开发区后巧报路
国家税务总局辽宁省税务局	刘 伟	024-23185436	辽宁省沈阳市沈河区青年大街256号
国家税务总局吉林省税务局	柴劲松	0431-80500257	吉林省长春市南湖大路1518号
国家税务总局黑龙江省税务局	邓黎明	0451-53611059	黑龙江省哈尔滨市南岗区大成街116号
国家税务总局上海市税务局	朱俊薇	021-54679568	上海市肇嘉浜路800号
国家税务总局江苏省税务局	倪 刚	025-58528531	江苏省南京市鼓楼区浦江路30号
国家税务总局浙江省税务局	王 真	0571-85270907	浙江省杭州市华浙广场5号
国家税务总局安徽省税务局	丁佳佳	0551-62831710	安徽省合肥市滨湖区中山路3398号

China Advance Pricing Arrangement Annual Report (2020)

VII STA Contacts (by Province) for APA Requests

Organization	Name	Telephone	Address
STA Headquarters	TIAN Chuan	010-63410887	No.1 Caiyuan Street, Xicheng District, Beijing
Beijing Municipal Tax Service, STA	MA Xiaowen	010-60907182	No.72(A) Tiantan Donglu, Dongcheng District, Beijing
Tianjin Municipal Tax Service, STA	WANG Chundi	022-24465656	No.16 Minzhu Street, Hebei District, Tianjin
Hebei Provincial Tax Service, STA	MA Zhenyu	0311-88625325	No.35 Ping'annan Street, Shijiazhuang, Hebei
Shanxi Provincial Tax Service, STA	YANG Jin	0351-2387616	No. 31 Shuiximen Street, Taiyuan, Shanxi
Inner Mongolia Autonomous Region Tax Service, STA	SUI Hongfeng	0471-3309112	Houqiaobao Street, Jinqiao Development Zone, Huhehaote, Inner Mongolia
Liaoning Provincial Tax Service, STA	LIU Wei	024-23185436	No.256 Qingnian Street, Shenhe District, Shenyang, Liaoning
Jilin Provincial Tax Service, STA	CHAI Jinsong	0431-80500257	No.1518 Nanhu Street, Changchun, Jilin
Heilongjiang Provincial Tax Service, STA	DENG Liming	0451-53611059	No.116 Dacheng Street, Nangang District, Haerbin, Heilongjiang
Shanghai Municipal Tax Service, STA	ZHU Junwei	021-54679568	No.800 Zhaojiabang Road, Shanghai
Jiangsu Provincial Tax Service, STA	NI Gang	025-58528531	No.30 Pujiang Road, Gulou District, Nanjing, Jiangsu
Zhejiang Provincial Tax Service, STA	WANG Zhen	0571-85270907	No.5 Huazhe Square, Hangzhou, Zhejiang
Anhui Provincial Tax Service, STA	DING Jiajia	0551-62831710	No.3398 Zhongshan Road, Binhu District, Hefei, Anhui

续表

单位	联系人	联系电话	联系地址
国家税务总局福建省税务局	潘晓耿	0591-87098271	福建省福州市铜盘路36号
国家税务总局江西省税务局	万海芳	0791-86204349	江西省南昌市红谷滩新区红谷南大道456号
国家税务总局山东省税务局	李振东	0531-85656421	山东省济南市英雄山路155号
国家税务总局河南省税务局	杨丽云	0371-66767708	河南省郑州市丰产路111号
国家税务总局湖北省税务局	马晓鸣	027-87322426	湖北省武汉市武昌区姚家岭路231号
国家税务总局湖南省税务局	周智勇	0731-85525533	湖南省长沙市雨花区环保西路6号
国家税务总局广东省税务局	朱国强	020-37990525	广东省广州市天河区花城大道767号
国家税务总局广西壮族自治区税务局	陈朝婷	0771-5562236	广西壮族自治区南宁市民族大道105号
国家税务总局海南省税务局	王凯霞	0898-66509357	海南省海口市龙昆北路10号
国家税务总局重庆市税务局	杜文渊	023-67572815	重庆市渝北区西湖路9号
国家税务总局四川省税务局	任荟宇	028-85458860	四川省成都市武侯区临江东路3号
国家税务总局贵州省税务局	颜红宇	0851-85215543	贵州省贵阳市中山西路71号
国家税务总局云南省税务局	兰 乐	0871-63129989	云南省昆明市盘龙区白塔路304号
国家税务总局西藏自治区税务局	谯海军	0891-6834079	西藏自治区拉萨市北京中路51号
国家税务总局陕西省税务局	赵 婷	029-87695187	陕西省西安市碑林区二环南路西段39号

(Continued)

Organization	Name	Telephone	Address
Fujian Provincial Tax Service, STA	PAN Xiaogeng	0591-87098271	No.36 Tongpan Road, Fuzhou, Fujian
Jiangxi Provincial Tax Service, STA	WANG Haifang	0791-86204349	No.456 Honggunan Road, Honggutan New District Nanchang, Jiangxi
Shandong Provincial Tax Service, STA	LI Zhendong	0531-85656421	No.155 Yingxiongshan Road, Jinan, Shandong
Henan Provincial Tax Service, STA	YANG Liyun	0371-66767708	No.111 Fengchan Road, Zhengzhou, Henan
Hubei Provincial Tax Service, STA	MA Xiaoming	027-87322426	No.231 Yaojialing Road, Wuchang District, Wuhan, Hubei
Hunan Provincial Tax Service, STA	ZHOU Zhiyong	0731-85525533	No.6 Huanbaoxi Road, Yuhua District Changsha, Hunan
Guangdong Provincial Tax Service, STA	ZHU Guoqiang	020-37990525	No.767 Huacheng Avenue, Tianhe District, Guangzhou, Guangdong
Guangxi Zhuang Autonomos Region Tax Service, STA	CHEN Zhaoting	0771-5562236	No.105 Minzu Avenue, Nanning, Guangxi
Hainan Provincial Tax Service, STA	WANG Kaixia	0898-66509357	No. 10 Longkunbei Road, Haikou, Hainan
Chongqing Municipal Tax Service, STA	DU Wenyuan	023-67572815	No.9 Xihu Road, Yubei District, Chongqing
Sichuang Provincial Tax Service, STA	REN Huiyu	028-85458860	No.3 Linjiangdong Road, Wuhou District, Chengdu, Sichuan
Guizhou Provincial Tax Service, STA	YAN Hongyu	0851-85215543	No.71 Zhongshanxi Road, Guiyang, Guizhou
Yunnan Provincial Tax Service, STA	LAN Le	0871-63129989	No.304 Baita Road, Panlong District Kunming, Yunnan
Tibet Autonomous Region Tax Service, STA	QIAO Haijun	0891-6834079	No.51 Beijingzhong Road, Lhasa, Tibet
Shaanxi Provincial Tax Service, STA	ZHAO Ting	029-87695187	No.39 Erhuannan Road, Xi'an, Shaanxi

续表

单位	联系人	联系电话	联系地址
国家税务总局甘肃省税务局	宋炜霞	0931-8837625	甘肃省兰州市城关区静宁路156号
国家税务总局青海省税务局	马满馨	0971-8220441	青海省西宁市城中区文化街11号
国家税务总局宁夏回族自治区税务局	王 丽	0951-5065733	宁夏回族自治区银川市金凤区北京中路161号
国家税务总局新疆维吾尔自治区税务局	曹佩浩	0991-2681362	新疆维吾尔自治区乌鲁木齐市天山区青年路397号
国家税务总局大连市税务局	马媛媛	0411-84384036	大连市沙河口区高尔基路330号
国家税务总局青岛市税务局	焦 娜	0532-83931089	青岛市延安三路236号
国家税务总局厦门市税务局	陈巩皓	0592-2021901	厦门市鹭江道318号鹭滨大厦
国家税务总局宁波市税务局	吴敏儿	0574-87732286	宁波市鄞州区百丈路8号
国家税务总局深圳市税务局	赵静怡	0755-25843846	深圳市福田区八卦二路613栋

(Continued)

Organization	Name	Telephone	Address
Gansu Provincial Tax Service, STA	SONG Weixia	0931-8837625	No.156 Jingning Road, Chengguan District, Lanzhou, Gansu
Qinghai Provincial Tax Service, STA	MA Manxin	0971-8220441	No.11 Wenhua Street, Xining, Qinghai
Ningxia Hui Autonomous Region Tax Service, STA	WANG Li	0951-5065733	No.161 Beijingzhong Road, Jinfeng District, Yinchuan, Ningxia
Xinjiang Uygur Automomous Region Tax Service, STA	CAO Peihao	0991-2681362	No.397 Qingnian Road, Tianshan District, Urumchi, Xinjiang
Dalian Tax Service, STA	MA Yuanyuan	0411-84384036	No.330 Gaoerji Road, Shahekou District, Dalian, Liaoning
Qingdao Tax Service, STA	JIAO Na	0532-83931089	No.236 Yanansan Road, Qingdao, Shandong
Xiamen Tax Service, STA	CHEN Gonghao	0592-2021901	No.318 Lujiang Road, Xiamen, Fujian
Ningbo Tax Service, STA	WU Miner	0574-87732286	No.8 Baizhang Road, Yinzhou District, Ningbo, Zhejiang
Shenzhen Tax Service, STA	ZHAO Jingyi	0755-25843846	No.613 Baguaer Road, Futian District, Shenzhen, Guangdong

附录：预约定价安排表证单书

附录1

预约定价安排预备会谈申请书

_____税务局：

根据

☐《中华人民共和国企业所得税法》及其实施条例

☐《中华人民共和国税收征收管理法》及其实施细则

☐ 中华人民共和国（政府）与_____（政府）间签订并执行的避免双重征税协定、协议或者安排

的有关规定，现就我企业与关联方之间的业务往来，提出

☐ 单边预约定价安排预备会谈申请

☐ 双边预约定价安排预备会谈申请

☐ 多边预约定价安排预备会谈申请

联系人：

联系电话：

附报资料：共　　份　　页

1._____

2._____

3._____

……

　　　　　　　　　　企业名称（盖章）：

　　　纳税人识别号（统一社会信用代码）：

　　　　　　　　　　法定代表人（签章）：

　　　　　　　　　　　　　　　年　月　日

China Advance Pricing Arrangement Annual Report (2020)

Appendices: Forms and Schedules of the APA Program

Appendix 1

APA Pre-filing Meeting Application Letter

_____ :

In accordance with:

☐ The *Law of the People's Republic of China on Enterprise Income Tax* and its Implementation Regulations;

☐ The *Law of the People's Republic of China on the Administration of Tax Collection* and its Implementation Regulations;

☐ The relevant provisions in the tax treaty entered into by the government of the People's Republic of China and the government of _____

for the transaction(s) between our Enterprise and our related party(ies), we apply for:

☐ Pre-filing Meeting (unilateral APA);

☐ Pre-filing Meeting (bilateral APA);

☐ Pre-filing Meeting (multilateral APA);

Contact person: _____ Contact telephone number _____.

Enclosures: Total ___ copies ___ pages

1. _____
2. _____
3. _____
...

Name of Enterprise (Official Stamp):

Taxpayer Identification Number:

Legal Representative (Official Stamp):

(Date):

附录2

预约定价安排谈签意向书

_____税务局：

　　根据

　　□《中华人民共和国企业所得税法》及其实施条例

　　□《中华人民共和国税收征收管理法》及其实施细则

　　□ 中华人民共和国（政府）与_____（政府）间签订并执行的避免双重征税协定、协议或者安排

的有关规定，按照你局_____年____月____日送达我企业的《税务事项通知书》（____税意向〔　　〕　　号）的要求，现就我企业与关联方_____（关联企业或者个人全称）之间的业务往来，提出

　　□ 单边预约定价安排谈签意向

　　□ 双边预约定价安排谈签意向

　　□ 多边预约定价安排谈签意向

　　请予签收。

　　附报资料：共　　份　　页

　　1._____

　　2._____

　　3._____

　　……

　　　　　　　　　企业名称（盖章）：
　　　　　　纳税人识别号（统一社会信用代码）：
　　　　　　　　　法定代表人（签章）：
　　　　　　　　　　　　　　年　　月　　日

Appendix 2

APA Letter of Intent

_____:

In accordance with:

☐ The *Law of the People's Republic of China on Enterprise Income Tax* and its Implementation Regulations;

☐ The *Law of the People's Republic of China on the Administration of Tax Collection* and its Implementation Regulations;

☐ The relevant provisions in the tax treaty entered into by the government of the People's Republic of China and the government of _____,

and in accordance with the requirements in the *Notice on Tax Matters* (_____ Shui Yi Xiang 〔　〕 No.　) issued by your bureau on _____ (Date), we apply for:

☐ Intention for unilateral APA;

☐ Intention for bilateral APA;

☐ Intention for multilateral APA;

for the transaction(s) between our Enterprise and _____ (name of the related party). Please sign and acknowledge receipt of this application.

Enclosures: Total ____ copies ____ pages

1. _____

2. _____

3. _____

…

Name of Enterprise (Official Stamp):

Taxpayer Identification Number:

Legal Representative (Official Stamp):

(Date):

附录3

预约定价安排正式申请书

_____税务局：

根据

□《中华人民共和国企业所得税法》及其实施条例

□《中华人民共和国税收征收管理法》及其实施细则

□ 中华人民共和国（政府）与_____（政府）间签订并执行的避免双重征税协定、协议或者安排

的有关规定，按照你局_____年____月____日送达我企业的《税务事项通知书》（____税预约〔   〕   号）的要求，现就我企业与关联方_____（关联企业或者个人全称）之间的业务往来，提出

□ 单边预约定价安排正式申请

□ 双边预约定价安排正式申请

□ 多边预约定价安排正式申请

请予签收。

附报资料：共   份   页

1._____

2._____

3._____

……

企业名称（盖章）：

纳税人识别号（统一社会信用代码）：

法定代表人（签章）：

年   月   日

China Advance Pricing Arrangement Annual Report (2020)

APA Formal Application Letter

_____:

In accordance with:

☐ The *Law of the People's Republic of China on Enterprise Income Tax* and its Implementation Regulations;

☐ The *Law of the People's Republic of China on the Administration of Tax Collection* and its Implementation Regulations;

☐ The relevant provisions in the tax treaty entered into by the government of the People's Republic of China and the government of _____,

and in accordance with the requirements in the *Notice on Tax Matters* (_____ Shui Yu Yue 〔   〕 No.   ) issued by your bureau on _____ (Date), we apply for:

☐ Formal application for unilateral APA;

☐ Formal application for bilateral APA;

☐ Formal application for multilateral APA;

for the transaction(s) between our Enterprise and the _____ (name of the related party). Please sign and acknowledge receipt of this application.

Enclosures: Total ___ copies ___ pages

1. _____

2. _____

3. _____

…

Name of Enterprise (Official Stamp):

Taxpayer Identification Number:

Legal Representative (Official Stamp):

(Date):

附录4

单边预约定价安排

(参照文本)

根据《中华人民共和国企业所得税法》及其实施条例和《中华人民共和国税收征收管理法》及其实施细则的有关规定，经＿＿＿＿＿＿（企业）正式申请，＿＿＿＿税务局审确认，双方愿意签署本预约定价安排。

第一条　一般定义

在本预约定价安排中，除上下文另有解释的以外：

（一）"主管税务机关"是指＿＿＿＿＿税务局。

（二）"纳税人"是指＿＿＿＿＿＿＿（企业），纳税人识别号（统一社会信用代码）＿＿＿＿＿＿＿＿＿＿＿，地址＿＿＿＿＿＿＿＿＿＿＿＿＿＿＿＿＿＿＿。

第二条　适用范围

（一）税种范围：本预约定价安排适用所得税以及其他税种。

（二）企业与其关联方之间业务往来类型：本预约定价安排适用于企业与其关联方＿＿＿＿＿＿＿之间的＿＿＿＿＿＿业务往来。

第三条　适用期间

本预约定价安排适用于＿＿＿＿年至＿＿＿＿年共＿＿个纳税年度，每一纳税年度自＿＿月＿＿日至＿＿月＿＿日。

第四条　关键假设

本预约定价安排选用的定价原则和计算方法是基于以下假设条件：

Advance Pricing Arrangement (Unilateral)

(Text for Reference)

Pursuant to the *Law of the People's Republic of China on Enterprise Income Tax* and its Implementation Regulations as well as the *Law of the People's Republic of China on the Administration of Tax Collection* and its Implementation Regulations, upon formal application of _____(company name) and the confirmation of the Tax Bureau of _____(tax office name), both parties would like to conclude this Advance Pricing Arrangement (hereinafter referred to as this "APA").

Article 1 General Definitions

For the purposes of this APA, unless otherwise defined elsewhere:
The term "in-charge tax authority" refers to the Tax Bureau of _____(tax office name).
The term "taxpayer" refers to _____(company name); Taxpayer Identification Number: _____;
Address: _____.

Article 2 Scope of Application

Type of tax(es) covered: This APA is applicable to enterprise income tax and other tax types.
Type of related party transaction(s) covered: This APA is applicable to _____(description of the transaction type) transactions between the taxpayer and _____(company name), which is its related party.

Article 3 Applicable Term

This APA is applicable for _____ year to _____ year, totally _____ (number) tax years. Each taxable year is from ____(month) ____(day) to ____(month) ____(day).

Article 4 Critical Assumptions

The transfer pricing methodology and calculation method used in this APA are based on the following assumptions:

_____
_____

在执行期内，若上述假设条件发生变化，企业应在发生变化30日内向主管税务机关报告，双方视具体情况修订或终止本预约定价安排。

第五条　转让定价方法

_____（企业）与其关联方之间_____（关联交易）采用的转让定价原则和计算方法为_____。（每一关联交易分别列明）

第六条　年度报告

在预约定价安排适用期间，企业应在每个纳税年度终了后六个月内提交预约定价安排执行情况的年度报告，并提交如下资料：

_____

第七条　预约定价安排的效力

在本预约定价安排适用期间，双方均应遵照执行。如果企业没有遵照执行，主管税务机关可视具体情况进行处理，或单方终止本预约定价安排。

第八条　预约定价安排的续签

本预约定价安排不作为续签的依据。企业应当按照有关规定提出续签申请。

第九条　争议的解决

如双方就本预约定价安排的实施和解释发生歧义，应先协商解决。经协商不能解决的，双方均可向上一级税务机关申请协调；预约定价安排同时涉及两个或者两个以上省、自治区、直辖市和计划单列市税务机关的，双方均可向国家税务总局申请协调。如果企业不能接受协调结果，可以考虑修订或终止本预约定价安排。

During the covered period, in case any of the above critical assumptions should change, the taxpayer should report to the in-charge tax authority within 30 days after the change takes place. Depending on the circumstances, the in-charge tax authority and the taxpayer may amend or terminate this APA.

Article 5 Transfer Pricing Method

The transfer pricing principle and calculation method used in this APA for the _____ transactions between _____ (company name) and its related party(ies) is _____ (Each related transaction should be separately listed).

Article 6 Annual Compliance Report

During the covered period of the APA, the taxpayer should file annual compliance reports in relation to the implementation situation of the APA within 6 months after the end of the taxable year, together with the following documents:

Article 7 Legal Binding Force of this APA

During the covered period of this APA, both of the tax authority and the taxpayer should complies with all the articles and requirements set out in this APA. If the taxpayer fails to comply with this APA, the in-charge tax authority may take actions according to the specific circumstances, or unilaterally terminate this APA.

Article 8 Renewal of this APA

This APA cannot be the basis to renew. The taxpayer should comply with relevant regulations to apply for renewal of APA.

Article 9 Dispute Resolution

In the event of disputes over the implementation and interpretation of this APA, the in-charge tax authority and the taxpayer should first negotiate to resolve such issues. If the disputes cannot be resolved through negotiation, both parties may petition the upper level tax authority for mediation; Where an APA involves two or more provinces, autonomous regions, municipalities directly under the central government or cities specifically designated in the state plan, both parties may petition the State Taxation Administration for mediation. If the taxpayer cannot accept the mediation resolution, it should consider revising or terminating this APA.

第十条　保密义务和责任

主管税务机关与企业在本预约定价安排的谈签及执行过程中获取的信息，双方均负有保密义务。

国家税务总局可以按照有关规定与其他国家（地区）税务主管当局就单边预约定价安排文本实施信息交换（涉及国家安全的信息除外）。

第十一条　生效、修订与终止

本预约定价安排自双方法定代表人或其授权人签字盖章后生效。

由主管税务机关和企业的法定代表人或者其授权代表于＿＿＿＿年＿＿月＿＿日在＿＿＿＿＿＿＿＿＿＿签署本预约定价安排。

主管税务机关或企业修订或终止预约定价安排，均应书面通知对方。通知内容包括修订或终止时间及原因。

第十二条　附　　则

本预约定价安排应当使用中文，一式＿＿＿份，主管税务机关和企业各执一份。

＿＿＿＿＿＿＿＿税务局　　　　　　　　　　＿＿＿＿＿＿＿＿（企业）

签名：　　　日期：　　　　　　　　签名：　　　日期：

职务：　　　盖章：　　　　　　　　职务：　　　盖章：

Article 10 Confidentiality and Responsibility

Both the in-charge tax administration(s) and the taxpayers are legally bound to keep the information and documents obtained through the APA process confidential.

The STA may exchange information on unilateral APAs with relevant competent authorities of other countries (regions) pursuant to the relevant international conventions, treaties, agreements between China and other countries (regions) unless the information concerns national security.

Article 11 Effectiveness, Amendment and Termination

This APA will come into effect once signed and stamped by the legal or authorized representatives of both parties.

This APA is signed by the legal or authorized representatives of the in-charge tax authority and the taxpayer in _____ (city), (province) on _____ (day-month-year).

If the in-charge tax authority or the taxpayer amends or terminates this APA, the party should notify the other party. The notification should include the time of and the reason for the amendment or termination in written form.

Article 12 Supplementary Provisions

This APA should be prepared in Chinese, in _____ (number) copies, one for the in-charge tax authority and the other for the taxpayer.

_____Tax Authority   _____ (Enterprise)

Signature: Date: Signature: Date:

Title: Stamp: Title: Stamp:

附录5

_____税务局
预约定价安排补（退）税款通知书

_____税预调〔   〕   号

_____（企业名称）：

根据

☐ 我局与你企业于_____年____月__日签署的_____（单边预约定价安排名称）

☐ 中国税务主管当局与_____税务主管当局于_____年____月__日签署的_____

_____（双边或者多边预约定价安排名称）

的有关规定，对你企业自_____年至_____年的纳税年度进行如下调整：

1. 调增（减）你企业应纳税所得额_____元，应补（退）企业所得税_____元，并按规定加收利息；

2. 调增（减）你企业应纳税收入_____元，应补（退）_____税_____元；

……

需要补缴税款的，你企业应当自收到本通知书之日起_____日内，向_____税务局缴纳上述税款及利息。逾期未缴纳税款的，按照《中华人民共和国税收征收管理法》有关规定执行。

特此通知。

附：1. 企业所得税调整项目表

2. 其他税种调整项目表

3. 各项税收应补（退）明细表

税务机关（公章）：

年   月   日

Appendix 5

_____ Tax Authority

Notice on APA Tax Payable (Refundable)

_____ Shui Yu Tiao 〔   〕 No. _____

_____ (name of taxpayer):

In accordance with

☐ The _____ (name of unilateral APA) signed on ____ (date-month-year) between our office and your company;

☐ The _____ (name of bilateral or multilateral APA) signed on _____ (date-month-year) between Tax authority of China and _____ (name of the competent authority of the tax treaty contracting party),

the taxable year from ____ to ____ will be adjusted:

1. Make a upward (downward) adjustment to the taxable income for ____ RMB, correspondingly paying (refunding) enterprise income tax for ____ RMB and surcharging interest as stipulated.

2. Make a upward (downward) adjustment to the assessable income for ____ RMB, correspondingly paying (refunding) ____ (tax category) for ____ RMB.

…

If additional tax payments were required, you have to pay the tax and interest to ____ (tax authority) within ____ days after receiving this notice. The late payment will be punished in accordance with the *Law of People's Republic of China on the Administration of Tax Collection*.

Hereby notified.

Attachments: 1. Enterprise Income Tax Adjustment Items
　　　　　　 2. Other Tax(es) Adjustment Items
　　　　　　 3. The Schedule of tax Payable(refundable)

　　　　　　　　　　　　　　　　　　　　Tax Authority (Stamp)
　　　　　　　　　　　　　　　　　　　　　　　　(Date)

附录6

预约定价安排续签申请书

_____税务局：

☐ 我企业与你局于_____年____月____日签署的_____（单边预约定价安排名称）

☐ 中国税务主管当局与_____税务主管当局于_____年____月____日签署的_____（双边或者多边预约定价安排名称）

将于_____年____月____日适用期满，期满后，拟就未来年度（即_____年度至_____年度）与关联方之间的业务往来提出续签申请。

企业名称（盖章）：

纳税人识别号（统一社会信用代码）：

法定代表人（签章）：

年　　月　　日

附：1. 执行现行预约定价安排情况的报告（纳税人提供）；

　　2. 现行预约定价安排所述事实和经营环境未发生实质性变化的说明材料以及续签预约定价安排年度的预测情况（纳税人提供）。

China Advance Pricing Arrangement Annual Report (2020)

APA Renewal Application

_____Tax Authority:

☐ The _____ (name of unilateral APA) signed on _____ (date-month-year) between your office and our company _____

☐ The _____ (name of bilateral APA) signed on _____ (date-month-year) between Tax authority of China and _____ (name of the competent authority(ies) of the tax treaty contracting party)

will expire on _____ (date-month-year). After expiration, our company plans to apply for APA renewal of related party transactions in the future years (from _____ to _____).

Name of Enterprise (Official Stamp):

Taxpayer Identification Number:

Legal Representative (Official Stamp):

(Date):

Attachments: 1. The annual APA implementation reports for the existing APA (provided by taxpayers).

2. The documents explaining whether there have been any substantial changes to the facts and operating environment specified in the existing APA, and forecast for the year to be covered by the APA renewal (provided by taxpayers).

附录7

启动特别纳税调整相互协商程序申请表

申请人基本情况	在中国	名称（中英文）	
		详细地址（中英文）	邮编
		纳税人识别号（统一社会信用代码）	
		联系人（中英文）	
		联系方式（电话、传真、电邮）	
		主管税务机关及其地址	邮编
		主管税务机关联系人	
		主管税务机关联系方式（电话、传真、电邮）	
		是否向中国申请了其他形式的国内救济，如行政复议或者行政诉讼？如是，请说明递交申请的时间，中国接受申请的时间，以及国内救济进展情况。	
申请人关联方或者相关方基本情况	在缔约对方	名称（中英文）	
		详细地址（中英文）	邮编
		税务登记号码	
		联系人（中英文）	
		联系方式（电话、传真、电邮）	
		缔约对方名称（中英文）	
		缔约对方主管当局及其地址（中英文）	
		缔约对方主管当局联系人（中英文）	
		缔约对方主管当局联系方式（电话、传真、电邮）	
		是否向缔约对方递交了相互协商程序申请？如是，请说明递交申请的时间以及缔约对方接受申请的时间。	
		是否向缔约对方申请了其他形式的国内救济，如行政复议或者行政诉讼？如是，请说明递交申请的时间，缔约对方接受申请的时间以及国内救济进展情况。	

Appendix 7

Application to Initiate Transfer Pricing Mutual Agreement Procedures

Basic information of the applicant	The party in China	Name (Chinese and English)	
		Detailed address (Chinese and English)	Postcode
		Taxpayer identification number	
		Contact Person (Chinese and English)	
		Contact information (telephone number, fax, email)	
		Name and address of the tax authority in charge (Chinese and English)	Postcode
		Contact Person of the tax authority in charge	
		Contact information (telephone number, fax, email) of the tax authority in charge	
		Whether to apply other domestic remedy or not? (e.g. Administrative Reconsideration, Administrative Proceeding) If so, please provide the submission date, the date that the application is accepted, and the progress of domestic remedy.	
Basic information of the related party(ies) of the applicant	The party in the other treaty partner	Name (Chinese and English)	
		Detailed address (Chinese and English)	Postcode
		Taxpayer identification number	
		Contact Person (Chinese and English)	
		Contact information (telephone number, fax, email) of the tax authority in charge	
		Name of the treaty partner (Chinese and English)	
		Detailed address of the tax authority in charge (Chinese and English)	
		Contact Person of the tax authority in charge (Chinese and English)	
		Contact information (telephone number, fax, email) of the tax authority in charge	
		Whether to submit the MAP application or not? If so, please provide the submission date and the date that the application is accepted by the treaty partner.	
		Whether to apply other domestic remedy or not? (e.g. Administrative Reconsideration, Administrative Proceeding) If so, please provide the date to submit application, the date that the application is accepted and the progress of domestic remedy.	

续表

申请相互协商事由概述	事实描述：	
	争议焦点：	
	申请人对争议焦点的观点以及依据	缔约对方对争议焦点的观点以及依据

附件清单（共　　件）：

声明：我谨郑重声明，本申请及其附件所提供的信息是真实的、完整的和准确的。我所提交的一切资料，除特别声明以外，均可以向缔约对方主管当局出示。我将配合缔约双方主管当局开展相互协商程序，并按其要求及时提供其所需信息。我了解并同意，相互协商程序仅在缔约双方主管当局授权代表间进行，我仅在缔约双方主管当局授权代表邀请时才可以参与。

声明人签章：

年　月　日

（注：申请人是个人的，由个人签字；申请人是法人或者其他组织的，由法定代表人或者负责人签字，并加盖单位印章。）

(Continued)

Summary of the issue to negotiate	Facts:	
	Issues:	
	The applicant's opinion on the issue and the relevant basis thereof	The opinion of the tax authority in charge in the other treaty country/region partner on the issue and the relevant basis thereof

Attachment list (Total items):

Declaration: I hereby declare that all the application and the attachment provided are truthful, complete and accurate. All the data I provided can be shown to the treaty partner except for those which are listed in the special announcement. I will support and cooperate both contracting parties to carry out mutual agreement procedure, and provide required information in time. I understand and agree that the mutual agreement procedure is only operated between the representatives of competent authorities of both contracting parties. Accordingly, Our company would take part in only when we are invited.

Signature of declarant:

Date(Day-Month-Year):

(Tips: For individual applicants, please sign your name; For corporate entities and other organizations, please appoint you legal representative or person in charge to sign and stamp)

附录8

单边预约定价安排简易程序申请书

_____税务局：

根据《中华人民共和国企业所得税法》及其实施条例、《中华人民共和国税收征收管理法》及其实施细则的有关规定，现就我企业与关联方_____（关联企业或者个人全称）之间的业务往来，提出单边预约定价安排简易程序申请，并附上以下附件。

附报资料：共　　份　　页

1._____

2._____

3._____

……

企业名称（盖章）：

纳税人识别号（统一社会信用代码）：

法定代表人（签章）：

年　　月　　日

Appendix 8

Application Letter for the Simplified Procedure for UAPA

_____ :

In accordance with the Law of the People's Republic of China on Enterprise Income Tax and its Implementation Regulations, and the Law of the People's Republic of China on the Administration of Tax Collection and its Implementation Regulations, we apply for the UAPA simplified procedure for the transaction(s) between our Enterprise and _____ (name of the related party).

Enclosures: Total ___ copies ___ pages

1. _____
2. _____
3. _____
…

Name of Enterprise (Official Stamp):

Taxpayer Identification Number:

Legal Representative (Official Stamp):

(Date):

图书在版编目（CIP）数据

中国预约定价安排年度报告. 2020：汉、英 / 中华人民共和国国家税务总局编. -- 北京：中国税务出版社，2021.9
ISBN 978-7-5678-1140-9

Ⅰ. ①中… Ⅱ. ①中… Ⅲ. ①税法—研究报告—中国—2020—汉、英 Ⅳ. ①D922.220.4

中国版本图书馆CIP数据核字（2021）第193294号

版权所有·侵权必究

书　　名：	中国预约定价安排年度报告（2020）
作　　者：	中华人民共和国国家税务总局　编
责任编辑：	范竹青
责任校对：	姚浩晴
技术设计：	刘冬珂
出版发行：	中国税务出版社

北京市丰台区广安路9号国投财富广场1号楼11层
邮政编码：100055
http：//www.taxation.cn
E-mail：swcb@taxation.cn
发行中心电话：（010）83362083 / 85 / 86
传真：（010）83362047 / 48 / 49

经　　销：	各地新华书店
印　　刷：	北京天宇星印刷厂
规　　格：	889毫米×1194毫米　1/16
印　　张：	6.5
字　　数：	106000字
版　　次：	2021年9月第1版　2021年9月第1次印刷
书　　号：	ISBN 978-7-5678-1140-9
定　　价：	28.00元

如有印装错误　本社负责调换